Missed Shifts

Missed Shifts

True stories, tall tales, and
outright lies from a 30-year
career in motojournalism

Jerry Smith

TREAD LIFE BOOKS

Design & production by Marcella Fox
MarcellaFox.com
Cover font family: Koblenz
Inside font families: American Typewriter and Baskerville

Contents

Introduction

My Accidental Career

For reasons I no longer remember, a few years ago I signed up with LinkedIn, which is Facebook for people with jobs—instead of posting pictures of your lunch, you post your resumé. Recently some nosy little LinkedIn bot sent out a notice to all of my connections—which is to say people in the motorcycle business I either know, or have merely heard of, or whose names I clicked on by accident—that I was "celebrating" my 30th anniversary as a freelance writer. Yippee. Three decades without a steady job. Good for me.

Oddly, this isn't the career path I started down in the first place. After high school I got a job in a motorcycle shop and figured I'd spend the rest of my days selling spark plugs and Torco two-stroke oil to kids with ratty DT1 Yamahas. Mercifully my life didn't pan out that way, and after a while I got a job at a motorcycle accessory distributor. All the while I was roadracing with the AFM in Northern California, and on weekends when I wasn't displaying my mediocre talents on pavement

I traipsed back home to the San Jose area where I snuck into flattrack races like the San Jose Mile and took photos that I eventually sold to *Cycle Guide* magazine, where—after a brief and chaotic stint at *Rider*—I became features editor in 1985.

Cycle Guide folded in 1987, and after six months of watching my bank account grow slimmer, I got a call from *Motorcyclist*'s editor, Art Friedman, inviting me to sit behind the desk recently vacated by Jeff Karr, who had been elevated to the editor's post at *Motor Trend*. Unemployment was fun but not very profitable, so I signed on. I lasted six months before the craziness of L.A. finally prompted me and my significant other to flee the smog and gridlock for the clean air of the Oregon coast, where her parents and family lived. There I began the freelance career I've beavered away at ever since.

Too much of what I've written since then has been the sort of work you do just for the money—product tests, news items, bike features, how-to articles, advertorial. It paid the bills but didn't nourish my mind, or demand much creativity. Now and then, though, I got to write something different—thoughtful, irreverent, from the heart. That's when the job was more than a job, and it's probably why I've kept doing it long past the time a reasonable person would have chucked it for a gig that came with a steady paycheck and benefits.

This book is a collection of that kind of writing. Some entries were done for money, others for my own amusement during a period when work was scarce and I needed to keep my spirits up. During that time I started a blog called Tread Life, and later another called Cycle Guide Magazine (CGM) with fellow freelancer and ex-*CG*er Dain Gingerelli.

For the kind permission to reprint some of these pieces I thank Mark Tuttle, editor-in-chief of *Rider*, and Patrick George, editor of the website Jalopnik. The rest are from Tread Life, CGM, and the murky depths of my own mind. Some pieces have been lightly edited to remove errors that escaped my notice the first time round, or references that don't make sense outside of the confines of the medium in which they first appeared, or because I felt like it.

When We Were Stupid

(TREAD LIFE, 2008)

"You know," Larry said, "I think I enjoyed motorcycles a lot more when I didn't know anything about them."

I was talking on the phone to a buddy who has an FXRS Harley. He's been thinking about replacing it with a Road King, and during one of our lengthy conversations on the merits of the swap, we got to talking about the days, years ago, when we both rode Honda CB350 twins and thought they were pretty neat bikes.

I had spent the day hanging bells and whistles on my 1200 Bandit. So far the list of frills on that bike—things I never dreamed existed back in my CB350 days—includes heated handgrips, an automatic chain oiler, auxiliary driving lights, a CB radio, three hard bags each big enough to stuff a goat in, and a power cord for my electric jacket liner and gloves. A radar detector and a microwave oven are in the works.

Back in the days when I didn't know much about motorcycles—or anything else—in about 1971 or so, another buddy of mine, coincidentally also named Jerry, and I saddled up our bikes, his a 500cc Suzuki Titan and mine a 350cc Yamaha R5, and rode from the San Francisco Bay Area to Los Angeles. The purpose of our trip was to visit the offices of the U.S. distributors of the big four Japanese brands, which all had their headquarters in Southern California. We had some fuzzy notion there would be tours on the hour, and exhibits, and test-rides on new bikes, and maybe even free key fobs, and we fully expected to return home brimming with tales of glory guaranteed to permanently inflame our friends' envy glands.

My entire collection of motorcycle luggage began and ended with a pair of vinyl throw-over saddlebags that cost $9.95. I lashed them to the Yamaha's seat with a couple of bungee cords, and crammed the left-side bag full of tools, chain lube, shop rags, a couple of spare inner tubes, (no tire irons, though), and a spare master link. The other side held some clothes, some more tools, some more shop rags, and a quart of Torco two-stroke oil.

My riding gear consisted of a jacket nearly identical to the one Fonzie later made famous, and a pair of 20-pound (each) engineer's boots purchased at The Workingman's Store, a pair of buckskin work gloves from Orchard Supply Hardware, blue jeans, a Buco open-face helmet, and Fuji Penguin goggles. I couldn't tell you now what I expected to wear in case it rained. I probably couldn't have told you then, either.

I have no memory of the trip to L.A., not the route we took or any of the stops along the way. When we arrived, we took up residence in a motel in Buena Park, near Knott's Berry Farm and right across the street from a Denny's. As soon as we unpacked we began mapping out the quickest way to each of the brands we wanted to visit. The first one we went to was Suzuki. As we pulled into the parking lot in front of the building, our imaginations furnished it with wonders the likes of which we had never seen in our short, innocent lives.

The astonished receptionist couldn't decide whether to take us home and feed us a hot meal, or call security. She looked at us like we were a couple of pimply-faced, dumb-ass kids—which we were—and patiently explained that, no, there were no tours. There was nothing to tour, unless we wanted to look at the accounting department, or the shipping dock, or the employee snack bar, and we weren't allowed to look at any of those things.

Undaunted, we tried Honda the next day. Same result. Yamaha and Kawasaki, ditto. No dream ever died a harder death. And the hell of it is, we really didn't care. We took in a half-mile at Ascot. We clomped around Disneyland looking like deserters from a rumble between the Sharks and the Jets. We were completely on our own for the first time in our lives. We could—and did—have Hostess SuzyQs and Coca-Cola for dinner whenever we felt like it. We had breakfast at Denny's so many times the cook started greeting us by name. We thought we were the two luckiest guys on the planet.

We took Highway 1 on the way home. The cold wind whistled up the sleeves of my jacket and right through the three sweaters I had on underneath it—windshields were for sissies. My hands went numb, and my brain nearly stopped working. We made Santa Cruz on the coast and turned inland. The weather warmed up—a lot. Now we were panting like whipped dogs, our overheated two-strokes pinging and surging as we crawled along in the sluggish beach traffic that stretched to the summit of twisty, dangerous Highway 17 and down into the Santa Clara Valley. By the time we got home that night we didn't have another mile left in us. And we would have turned right around and done it again the next day.

"Sounds like it was a real fun trip," Larry said over the phone.

"It was," I said, "although I doubt it would have been if I'd known about electric vests and fairings and rainsuits."

"Then it's a good thing you didn't know about them," Larry said.

"Yes," I replied. "Sometimes it's good to be stupid."

Craigslist Motorcycle Ads
Decoded

(TREAD LIFE, 2009)

"Ran when parked."...six years ago under the awning on the side of my motorhome with the gas cap open so the bad gas would evaporate.

"No title, but I have a bill of sale."...written on the back of a Taco Bell napkin. The seller's handwriting wasn't too good, so you can tell the DMV you bought it from me. I'll back you up if anybody asks.

"Very rare." Nobody bought them when they were new.

"Classic." They don't make parts for them any more.

"Starts with no problem."...unless kicking it over for 30 minutes is a problem.

"Minor surface rust." All minor surfaces are rusted.

"Don't need it any more." Don't want it any more.

"Don't ride any more." Buy this bike and you'll see why.

"Will consider trades." Anything has got to be better than this.

"Great commuter bike." Slow and dull.

"Gets great gas mileage." Uses a quart of oil every 100 miles.

"Perfect Christmas present." For me, if you pay cash.

"Never been dropped." Fell over by itself a few times.

"Tags good for two years." As soon as you pay for them.

That Time My Motorcycle Got Stolen

And how to keep it from happening to to you

(JALOPNIK, 2015)

The warehouse crew were good guys, but too fond of practical jokes. So when I glanced over at the lot where I'd parked my bike that morning and saw the empty space, I thought, *Those meatheads better not have scratched it*. But nobody fessed up to moving it, and a search of the warehouse—including that corner way in the back where they held Friday-night short-track races with forklifts—failed to turn up my bike. That's when I knew I'd been ripped off.

The numbers vary depending on the source, and they're not exactly up to date, but motorcycle theft statistics are depressing no matter when they're from. In 2012, more than 46,000 motorcycles were stolen, and the recovery rate was only about 40 percent. The top-five favorite brands among thieves were, in order, Honda, Yamaha, Suzuki, Kawasaki, and Harley-Davidson. (Yeah, I thought Harley would be first, too.) California in July topped the nation as the most likely place and time to have your bike stolen.

As it happened, my bike disappeared from the parking lot in July, outside where I worked at a large West Coast motorcycle accessory distributor in California, in 1982. That year's stats might have pinpointed another time and place as rip-off central, but from where I was standing I was at ground zero, with a two-wheeled hole in my life and no way to get home that afternoon. So I went to my office, called the cops, filed a report, and then rang all the motorcycle dealers, repair shops, and salvage yards in the area to be on the lookout for a silver Honda CB900F with a repainted Windjammer fairing.

The cops implied the likelihood of getting my bike back was about the same as recovering a stolen kiss. I had pretty much written it off after a week when one day at work the phone rang. It was Larry, who ran a salvage yard. "Remember that Windjammer I sold you last year?" he said. "The one that was on your bike when it got stolen? I just bought it off a guy."

Larry recognized the fairing as soon as he saw it. He had a poker face that would have made Doc Holliday look like Mr. Bean, and he maintained it while paying the guy $100 and making him sign a receipt and write down his address and phone number. "I knew that shitty paint job right off," he said.

I ducked out of work and drove over to Larry's shop. When I got there he was talking to a police detective. Horace Smith was a huge, wide man who, judging by the way his upper body strained the seams of his jacket, was made out of bricks. He had a weary, seen-it-all look on his face that said, "Is that all you got? Brother, I've seen worse. Much worse."

On his hip was a nickel-plated, short-barreled Colt Python .357, and I never doubted for an instant that he hit whatever he shot at. Horace made John Shaft look like Steve Urkel.

When Larry showed him the receipt, he lit up like a kid at Christmas. "Know this guy," he said. "Dealt with him before." What now? I said. "Gonna arrest him," Horace said, then he added, "Wanna ride along?"

I slid into the passenger seat of the big four-door cruiser that didn't have a single distinguishing mark on it and yet somehow looked exactly like a cop car. Inside it smelled of sweat and desperation. Traffic moved seamlessly out of its way like mackerel making room for a shark as we hit the Bayshore Freeway heading north.

For some reason Horace spent most of the ride trying to sell me on signing up for the California Highway Patrol academy in Sacramento and becoming a motor cop. It seemed imprudent to laugh in the face of such a large man packing an equally large gun, so instead I said I'd think about it.

We arrived at the guy's house and Horace told me to stay in the car. He walked up to the front porch, took out his gun and held it beside his leg, and standing to one side of the door reached over and knocked. A young woman answered, and after a short discussion shut the door again.

"Let's take a ride," Horace said as he climbed back into the car. We drove slowly around the neighborhood until we passed a young man walking the other way. Horace slammed on the brakes, did a U-turn, and went after him. "He's not wearing shoes," he said, "just socks."

When the doorbell rang the guy had panicked, crawled out a window, jumped the back fence, cut across the neighbor's yard, and come out on the street on the opposite side of the block while his girlfriend stalled Horace.

When we returned to the house with her man in cuffs in the back seat, she still wouldn't let Horace in. I watched from the front seat as Horace talked to her for about 15 minutes, giving her the "I can get a search warrant so you might as well open up" speech. Finally she went inside, and a moment later the garage door rose slowly.

Inside was an abattoir of motorcycles. Pieces of bikes—frames, engine cases, wheels, fenders—were scattered all over the oil-stained floor. In one corner was the frame of my bike, hacksawed into several pieces. Outside, in the walkway beside the garage, was my engine. The VIN had been obliterated with a hammer and chisel, and an excess of enthusiasm had cracked the crankcase.

A pair of riding gloves I kept in the pocket of the Windjammer sat on a workbench. I held them up to Horace. "Do you need these for anything? Evidence?" He shook his head. "We got enough here." I put them in my pocket. At least I'd have something left from all this.

Insurance eventually paid off the bike, and left me with enough for a down payment on another. After what I'd just been through I got serious about motorcycle theft prevention.

Well, that's what I'd like to say I did, but I kept on doing all the dumb things that make life easy for bike thieves. I've been lucky, but maybe you won't be. So here's what you need to do to tip the odds in your favor.

First, realize that if professional thieves want your bike badly enough, they'll get it. Lock it, alarm it, park it in an underground nuclear missile silo—doesn't matter, it's gone. But most amateur thieves are basically lazy, so the trick is to make your bike look like a harder target than the one parked next to it. Here's how:

• Use a lock. An unlocked bike is easy to steal, but almost any kind of lock takes time and tools to break, and someone hanging around your bike with a pair of bolt cutters is liable to attract attention. If nothing else a lock is a visual deterrent that shifts the odds in your favor.

• If you have an alarm that beeps loudly or signals you through a remote, answer the alert every time. Every. Damn. Time. Savvy bad guys trip the alarm and hang around to see if anyone responds. If you ignore it, so will the bad guy.

• Two or three prison-trained weightlifters can easily pick up your bike and toss it in a truck or van and be gone in a heartbeat—not even a beeping alarm will stop them. Chain or cable-lock it to something solid like a lamppost, or another motorcycle.

• Park your bike under a light or on a busy street, not down a dark alley where a thief can take his time ruining your day without being seen.

• A lot of bikes are stolen from garages where they're regularly parked. Sink a steel loop into the cement floor of your garage and secure your bike to it. Park your car so you have to move it to get the bike out.

• If none of these tricks works, and the worst happens, there's still a chance of recovering your bike. Engrave identifying numbers or letters on the back of side covers, under the seat, and on other parts that are easily removed and put on eBay or Craigslist. There's a chance one will turn up and lead you to the bastard who ripped you off.

• A shitty rattle-can paint job on a large aftermarket accessory is a long shot, but what the hell, it worked for me.

After Horace called someone out to collect the evidence from the guy's house, he drove us straight to the county jail to process him. He parked around back under a sign that said "Intake" and said he'd be gone about an hour. He told me to wait in the car, because wandering around a county jail for no apparent reason was a good way to see parts of it you didn't really want to see.

If you're ever ripped off, and the cop offers to take you along while he busts the perp, do it—it's pretty satisfying—but make sure you go to the bathroom first. By the time he came back to the car I would have gladly gotten myself thrown in a cell, as long as it had a toilet.

Family Ties

(TREAD LIFE, 2008)

Dad was an aircraft mechanic. He was born 10 years after the Wright Brothers flew, and dreamed of being a pilot himself someday. He passed all the tests but failed the eye exam. So he did the next best thing and got a job working on planes for companies like Vultee, Convair, and Pan Am, and finished out his career at NASA's Ames Research Center at Moffett Field Naval Air Station in Mountain View, California.

In his life he saw the Spruce Goose fly, worked on P-51 Mustangs bound for the war in the Pacific, and shook hands with Neil Armstrong, who was just back from the moon. Dad had big, rough-knuckled hands with thick blue veins running down the back, and if I close my eyes I can still see them turning a wrench, or sawing a board, or hammering a nail. To this day I use hand tools exactly the same way he did. Exactly.

We weren't the kind of father and son you see on old sitcoms, playing basketball in the driveway or working on cars together. We had fundamental differences of opinion about certain things. He thought Nixon was trying to save Vietnam from the Communists. I thought Nixon was trying to get me killed by the Communists. Dad wanted me to go to college, I wanted to go to the Daytona 200. It wasn't that we were mad at each other, it's just that we didn't have a lot to say to each other, and a lot of years passed between us in uneasy silence.

Once during those years, while I was out in the garage trying to graft a Yamaha RD350 front brake caliper to the Ceriani fork on my TD2B roadracer, he came in and asked what I was doing. As I explained, he squatted beside me, and with his ever-present translucent green mechanical pencil with "Property US Government" stamped on it he began making sketches on a piece of cardboard, taking several measurements with a small steel ruler he kept in his shirt pocket next to his pencil. Then he stood up, put the pencil and ruler and the sketches in his shirt pocket, and left.

A few hours later he returned with an aluminum bracket he had fabricated at the San Jose airport, where he moonlighted making radio cabinets for private pilots. It was a masterpiece of three-dimensional design, a single piece that spanned the distance between fork and caliper as economically and as elegantly as if da Vinci had dreamed it. Four marks with a center punch and another trip to the airport later, and mounting holes appeared exactly where they needed to be.

At the bike's—and my—professional roadrace debut, Harley-Davidson racing chief and certifiable legend Dick O'Brien stopped in his tracks to admire that bracket. For the next several years my life was metaphorically in my father's hands every time I grabbed the front brake in a race. I eventually sold the bike, kept the front end for its replacement, and finally sold that bike when I quit racing.

Dad got old, as men will, and needed a quadruple bypass. The years went by, and he needed another, only this time he didn't rebound from it the way he had the first time. When it became obvious there wasn't any point in occupying a hospital bed any longer, he moved into my sister's house to die. I was living a thousand miles away by then, and we tried to fill the gap that lay between us with frequent phone conversations. Of all the things we could have talked about, that bracket came up more often than not. It was our way of proving we were connected after all.

A month before he died I found a blurry photo of that old race bike, with the bracket barely visible on the off-side of the front wheel, and sent it to him. After he died, my sister told me he had kept it beside his bed, with his Bible and a few other treasures from a life well lived. I took a lot of his stuff home with me—his letter sweater from his track days in college, mementos of his work with NASA—but I never found that photo. My sister looked, too, and she never found it, either.

They say you can't take it with you. Maybe they're wrong.

The Crash That Made Me
Quit Racing

(JALOPNIK, 2015)

I came to in the infield, lying on sharp, baseball-sized rocks and gasping for air like a beached fish—all the ribs on my right side were broken and poking my insides as if I'd swallowed an opened Swiss army knife. I also had a dislocated shoulder, a torn rotator cuff, a broken collarbone, a fractured vertebra, and torn tendons. Pretty much all that held my right arm to the rest of my body was skin.

A sane person would have quit motorcycle racing on the spot. Not me, though. Not quite yet.

There's a saying you'll hear in almost every one of the speed sports: You're not in control unless you're a little bit out of control. What this means is if you're not scaring yourself a little, you're not going fast enough. But you don't have to go scary fast to lose control in racing. Sometimes control just walks away and turns you over to luck.

For a long time I was lucky, then I wasn't, and before my luck ran all the way out I decided to cut my losses and give up racing and track riding.

Hanging up my leathers wasn't easy—even a mediocre roadracer like me has some ego investment in being a go-fast guy—but by the time I realized I was entirely too familiar with the way hospital emergency rooms worked, quitting racing was the only choice that made sense.

By "racing" I don't just mean competing on a closed course, but riding stupid fast on the street, too. In the 1970s I lived in Marin County, California, and every week took part in the motorized lemming stampede known as the Sunday Morning Ride.

It began at an Arco station in Mill Valley where 10 or 20 or 80 bikes would gather in the morning mist and at 7 a.m. or so leave in a cloud of Castrol smoke and testosterone on a frenzied dash up twisty and treacherous Highway 1 toward a restaurant in Inverness where the first rider to arrive had the dubious honor of ordering before anyone else.

One morning I was wrestling my Ducati Darmah SS along a fast stretch of road with my buddy on his Honda CBX close behind. Ahead the road crested slightly, and in a sickening instant I realized I had no memory of which way the road went on the other side of the blind rise—left, right, or straight? I gambled on right, won, and trailed sparks from the Duck's Conti muffler all the way through the corner.

At breakfast my buddy slapped me on the back and said, "Smith, you were *flying* back there!" He didn't notice my face was still as white as a funeral shroud. It was a good thing I hadn't eaten yet or I'd have puked all over his Bates boots.

My pro racing career was uneventful, mostly because although I held a professional license, I was strictly an amateur with neither the talent nor the drive to hang it out too far. It was when I became a magazine writer that I got a good look at the other side of the edge—very nearly my last look at anything, ever.

On July 1, 1986, during a session at Willow Springs Raceway where *Cycle Guide* had assembled a collection of sportbikes to see which one was the best handling, I grabbed too much front brake coming off the main straight at about a buck-fifty, smoked the front tire, and head-butted Turn 1 so hard it knocked me out cold.

To this day my memory of that crash stops right before it all went pear-shaped. I was tucked in down the straight, sat up to brake, and then the next thing I knew I was on my back looking up at a paramedic who was asking me where it hurt. Everywhere, I said, and I meant it.

I spent a couple of weeks in various hospitals, and another couple of months recovering at home with a pin through my three-piece collarbone sticking out of my shoulder (I used to grab the hooked end and spin it around to show off). My right arm was draped over a piece of egg-crate foam as big as an old Sears sleeping bag and taped to my side.

Sleep was out of the question, along with coherent conversation thanks to the fistful of drugs I took every day to manage the pain and fight off the infection from a number of raw spots I'd gotten when my gloves flew off as I pinwheeled down the track.

I can't overemphasize how young and dumb I was at the time. Even before the pin in my collarbone came out I was sneaking in rides around the block on my '75 CB400F, making sure to be back in bed before my girlfriend got home from work.

In hindsight I have to wonder if the doctors missed some sort of traumatic brain injury, because four months after that, reasonably fit and back at work, I flew to France for the introduction of the 1987 Yamahas and found myself at Circuit Paul Ricard, clinging to the back of an FZR1000 as the speedo needle swung past the 160 mark in the middle of a straightaway so long I thought I'd have to stop for gas halfway down it.

I remember thinking, *If I fall off here for any reason I'll slide so far I'll be two-dimensional by the time I stop.* With that I parked the FZR and called it a day.

But then in March I arrived in Daytona to take part in the vintage races before the big race on Sunday. I had arranged to ride an immaculate 250cc Ducati single owned and built by an experienced vintage racer named Mike Green. The bike was as cute as a Golden Retriever puppy, although one with its feet on the wrong way around—the shifter was on the right, where Ducati put it, and not on the left, where it had been on every bike I'd ever ridden. Worse, the front brake was a drum about as big around as a tortilla, and with about the same coefficient of friction.

After a few laps of familiarization I knew I'd be lucky to finish the 10-lap race before everyone else had left the track for the day. I was spared that humiliation by some hot dog who was trying to win practice and dove under me in a corner and knocked the right clip-on out of my hand, sending me once again siding down a track face-first.

Having just come back from the Willow crash—which three doctors told me I was very lucky to have survived—I wasn't taking any chances. I stayed where I'd fallen on the track until the ambulance took me to Halifax Hospital, near the Speedway. I was wheeled into a room where two other riders who had been actually hurt lay breathing heavily and groaning softly.

I checked out fine except for a big, bloody chunk of road rash on the back of my hand where, again, a glove had come off as I slid. The first word of "emergency room" was apparently used here ironically because I sat there with my two fallen comrades for about an hour before I was able to hitch a ride in an ambulance back to the track.

By then I'd had plenty of time to think about racing, and the consequences of doing it less than perfectly. When I was in my 20s I believed I was invulnerable and immortal, as brave and foolish young men often do. The intervening years had given me cause to reconsider. I was 35, with a job I loved—but not enough to die for—and a woman I also loved and who had put her own life on hold to care for me the last time I'd mistaken enthusiasm for talent. I liked all that stuff a lot more than I enjoyed racing. I decided right then that Daytona would be the last track I ever rode on for any reason.

I've stuck to that ever since. If I'm ever tempted to break my deal with myself—and I'll admit there have been times—I have my mis-aligned ribs, my aching back, and my inability to walk in a straight line or throw a ball to remind me that being in control might not be the way to win, but it's a good way to make it to the finish alive.

The Riot And The Photo That Made Bikers Into Outlaws

(JALOPNIK, 2015)

Over the Fourth of July weekend in 1947, the American Motorcyclist Association Gypsy Tour rolled into the sleepy farming town of Hollister, California. By the time it rolled out, nothing would ever again be the same for motorcyclists, whom the non-riding public would forever afterward see through a lens clouded with black leather, big Harleys, beer, and bad behavior.

The small town, still reeling from the aftershocks of World War II with the rest of the country, played witness to violence, crashes, arrests, and destruction in an incident that many say cemented the "outlaw" image of the motorcyclist still prevalent in culture today. For motorcyclists, that weekend is known simply as Hollister.

Depending on who you talk to, Hollister is either a watershed event in the history of motorcycling, or a long-dead horse that some motorcyclists just can't stop beating. Whether it really turned the American public against motorcyclists, or merely served as a scapegoat for a problem that already existed long before the Gypsy Tour roared into that small California town in 1947, is a question that will never be settled for certain.

But the debate that still smolders 68 years later has been marked by both a scarcity of facts and a surplus of fancy. I had heard enough versions of the "truth" about Hollister over the years that when I was assigned to write a piece about it in 1994 for the inaugural issue of *American Rider*, I took to the task eagerly, and remained interested in the topic for long enough afterward to do some additional investigation.

First, some background: On the evening of Thursday, July 3, 1947, motorcyclists began arriving in Hollister for the annual Gypsy Tour, a three-day carnival of races and field events planned for the Fourth of July weekend. By the next day their numbers had swollen beyond expectations.

AMA officials said they had registered 1500 riders and that at least that many more had arrived but not registered. Later estimates of the number of riders in the town of 4900 varied, but the most frequently quoted figure was 4000.

By Saturday night the celebration began spilling over into the streets. The local hospital was jammed with injured bikers, and the police arrested so many revelers for a variety of offenses that a special session of night court was convened.

About 30 California Highway Patrol officers armed with tear-gas guns were called in to supplement the overmatched Hollister police force. Two blocks of the main drag, San Benito Avenue, were cordoned off and all but ceded to the motorcyclists. A band was summoned to play for them, and they danced amid discarded beer bottles. By Sunday, with the county jail bulging with hung-over lawbreakers, the party began to run out of steam. The last of the motorcyclists left after Monday's races, and life returned to something like normal in Hollister.

How bad was the Gypsy Tour? Did the police over-react? Did the press exaggerate the damage?

The question is so subjective that it borders on pointless. Remember that many of the young men who converged on Hollister that weekend arrived with the horrors of a world war still fresh in their memories. To someone who had stormed the beach at Normandy, or huddled in a foxhole on some flyspeck of sand in the Pacific, riding a motorcycle through the doors of a restaurant was nothing to get upset about.

To some of the folks on the home front, however, who had spent the war years tilling their fields, raising their children, and praying that the chaos devouring the world would spare their community, it couldn't have been any more terrifying if German tanks had come rolling down San Benito Avenue.

Less subjective is the question of whether, as is often claimed, the press unfairly exaggerated events. The primary source of information about that weekend was the local newspaper, the *Free Lance*, whose reporters were not only first on the scene, but fielded telephone calls from newspapers all across the country as word of the event spread.

In the late 1990s, back issues of the *Free Lance* were available on microfilm, so I ordered them up from my local library. From these reports I gleaned the essential details of the story that spread in the wake of the Gypsy Tour.

Next I ordered microfilm back issues of prominent national newspapers such as the *San Francisco Chronicle*, the *Los Angeles Times*, the *Chicago Daily Tribune*, and the *New York Times*. Not surprisingly, the farther the paper was from Hollister, the more perfunctory its accounts were.

In contrast to the multiday coverage in the *Free Lance* and the *Chronicle*, the *Chicago Daily Tribune* gave a total of 67 lines of copy to the story, the *Los Angeles Times* 60, and the *New York Times* a mere 43, and none ran photos. The tale did not grow in the telling, as I had often heard charged, but rather shrank, and the *Free Lance*'s account was, for the most part, accurately retold, not grossly exaggerated, in subsequent press reports.

The locals were divided in their reaction to the "invasion" of their town. "It has always been a pleasure to come to Hollister to shop—until I came over Saturday," wrote R.E. Stevenson of nearby Salinas in a letter to the editor of the *Free Lance*.

> The town was overrun with lawless, drunken, filthy bands of motorcycle fiends and it was impossible for law-abiding citizens to drive on your streets…drunks slept in the gutters…What is the matter with your city trustees that they allow such disgraceful happenings?

That earned this heated response from Mrs. Ruth Reynolds:

> R.E. Stevenson, our Salinas shopper, might well pick his hometown's skirts out of the mud before he writes any more letters to the editor….While he may have been offended by the somewhat noisy mob that cluttered up his personal shopping district, I wonder what his reactions were to the indescribable horror that roared up and down Main Street in Salinas on a Saturday night during the recent rodeo…If (motorcyclists) slept in the gutter they took an awful chance—some Salinas motorist might have run over them…It was noisy, often annoying, but was damage-free….

Just as the furor was dying down in Hollister, a single photograph fanned it back to life. The photo showed an apparently drunk biker on a Harley, a beer bottle in each hand and many more on the ground beneath his bike.

It appeared on page 31 (not on the cover, as is often claimed) of the July 21, 1947, issue of *Life* magazine, over the headline "Cyclists' Holiday," the subhead "He and friends terrorize a town," and the following caption:

> On the Fourth of July weekend 4,000 members of a motorcycle club roared into Hollister, California, for a three-day convention. They quickly tired of ordinary motorcycle thrills and turned to more exciting stunts. Racing their vehicles down the main street and through traffic lights, they rammed into restaurants and bars, breaking furniture and mirrors. Some rested by the curb. Others hardly paused. Police arrested many for drunkenness and indecent exposure but could not restore order. Finally, after two days, the cyclists left with a brazen explanation. "We like to show off. It's just a lot of fun." But Hollister's police chief took a different view. Wailed he, "It's just one hell of a mess."

Life's national distribution made sure that all of America got a good, long look at the drunk on the Harley. The photo, one of two that appeared in the *San Francisco Chronicle* on Monday, July 7, was taken in Hollister the previous Friday night by *Chronicle* photographer Barney Peterson. With the click of a shutter, motorcycling's worst nightmare became a reality. To many motorcyclists, that one stark, black-and-white image dealt a fatal blow to their cherished self-image.

Just as allegations of exaggeration were leveled at the press accounts of the Gypsy Tour, rumors that the photo was faked have survived to the present day. At first glance, there's nothing in the photo that is inconsistent with the general description of the events. There were certainly motorcycles in town that weekend. Police records show numerous arrests for drunkenness. And in the aftermath, city street sweepers reported hauling away at least half a ton of broken glass, mostly from beer bottles thrown in the street.

My early attempts to authenticate the photo were stymied by the fact that Barney Peterson had died a few years before. He was well remembered by his surviving colleagues at the *Chronicle*. "Barney was not the type to fake a picture," recalled Jerry Telfer, a photo assignment editor who knew Peterson. "Barney was the kind of fellow who had a very keen sense of ethics, pictorial ethics as well as word ethics."

I then shifted the focus of my search to try to discover the identity of the drunk on the bike. Peterson took less than a dozen photos in Hollister, only two of which appeared in the *Chronicle*. The rest sat in the photo morgue until they were published in a book called *Bikes: Motorcycles and the People Who Ride Them*, by Thierry Sagnier.

In this book a second photo of the drunk appears, this time with a jacket draped over his shoulder. Across the back of the jacket, partially obscured, is a patch that reads "Tulare Raiders" and "Dave" underneath.

I got back in touch with the *Chronicle* and spoke to a man there named Gary Fong. I asked him if Peterson had written down Dave's full name or any other information about him that might help me track him down.

Fong, who had already spoken to Jerry Telfer about the photo, said that he had "got back to the negative, and on the negative is the name Eddie Davenport." Fong added, "That's what photographers did with large-format, 4x5 negatives, they put it in ink or pencil. This one's in ink. After the negative's dried, and they're ready to archive it, they usually put the subject [on it]."

If the drunk on the Harley was in fact named Eddie Davenport, it increased the likelihood that the jacket he held in one of the pictures had been borrowed from someone named Dave—although it's interesting to note that the name Davenport contains the name Dave. A nickname, maybe?

The name Dave by itself wasn't enough to go on, so I concentrated on finding Eddie Davenport. I contacted the Tulare County Assessor's Office and found no record of an Eddie Davenport owning property in the county. I placed an ad in the local newspaper, the *Tulare Advanced Register*, seeking an Eddie Davenport who had attended the 1947 Gypsy Tour in Hollister; I also placed ads in papers in several adjoining areas, and sent flyers to a dozen or so motorcycle shops in the Central Valley.

Those ads and flyers had an unexpected result. Daniel Corral, Jr., a Hollister resident and a member of the San Benito County Historical Society, saw one of them and contacted me. He, too, was researching Hollister, and was also interested in the identity and whereabouts of Dave/Eddie Davenport.

Neither of us had come up with anything so far, but then Corral told me he knew the identity of the man in the *Life* photo who was standing on the sidewalk behind the drunk on the bike. That man's name was Gus De Serpa, and he still lived in Hollister. What's more, Corral said, De Serpa claimed to have watched Barney Peterson stage the photo.

In April of 1997, *American Rider* editor Buzz Buzzelli and I traveled to Hollister to talk to Gus De Serpa. He and his wife Mary Lou invited us to their home where Gus told us what he had seen that night.

De Serpa was working as a movie projectionist in the Granada Theatre on the night of Friday, July 4, 1947, and after his shift ended at 11 p.m. he walked over to San Benito Avenue to take in the spectacle the whole town was talking about.

"We went uptown, my former wife and I," recalled De Serpa, "to see all the excitement, and we ran into these people. They were on the sidewalk and there was a photographer. They started to scrape up the bottles with their feet, you know, from one side to another, and then they took the motorcycle and picked it up and set it right in the glass."

Of the man on the motorcycle, De Serpa said, "That's not his motorcycle, I can tell you that. He was just in the vicinity, and he was pretty well loaded. There was a bar right there, Johnny's Bar. I think he came wandering out of that bar, and they just got him to sit down there. I told my wife, 'That's not right; they shouldn't be doing that. Let's stand behind them so they won't take the picture.' I figured if I was behind them they wouldn't take it. But he took a picture anyhow, this fellow did, he didn't care. And then after that, everybody went on about their business."

De Serpa's testimony would seem to settle the matter of the photo's authenticity. At the same time, his recollection of the events of that night means it's unlikely we'll ever discover the true identity of the drunk. There never was any evidence that the bike in the photo was his—De Serpa was adamant that it wasn't—or that he was even a motorcyclist.

The jacket with the Tulare Raiders patch might have been borrowed from an onlooker, just as the motorcycle apparently had been. Dave/Eddie could just as easily have been a farm hand who was knocking back a few cold ones after a long day of riding a tractor, not a Harley, and who on leaving Johnny's Bar was asked by a man with a camera to sit on a motorcycle.

But does the fact that the photo was faked really change anything? To blame the events in Hollister, or the Barney Peterson photo, for the negative image that makes some motorcyclists squirm today is too simplistic.

If all motorcyclists had been model citizens before Hollister, it's unlikely that the public's perception of them would have been so drastically altered by an isolated incident. Nor would that incident alone have transformed sober, industrious motorcyclists into the kind of moody, unpredictable, beer-swilling thugs portrayed in movies like *The Wild One* and countless biker-gang B-movie stinkers.

In the years since I interviewed Gus De Serpa in 1997, I've spent more than a few idle hours thinking about all this, and I'm still not sure what to make of it. On one side is Jerry Telfer, a man who knew and worked with Barney Peterson, and who remembered him as an honest and ethical photojournalist.

On the other side is a man who said he saw Peterson staging what was probably the most well-known picture the photographer ever took, and whose claim is bolstered by his presence in the photo itself.

That's not the only question that remains unanswered. If the drunk on the Harley was in fact a motorcyclist named Eddie Davenport, why did he never come forward to tell the truth about the role he played in the famous photo?

For a long time I thought I'd never know. I originally wrote this piece about Hollister—which you're reading here substantially un-changed except for a few updates—on a blog in 2010. Then other work came along and I forgot about it.

When I happened to check that blog a year later I saw a comment had been left by someone who signed it "Garry E Clovis Ca." I had no luck tracking him down, but what he wrote seems to solve the mystery of the true identity of the biker in the Barney Peterson photo. This is what he wrote:

> I have read some of the info on this staged bike picture in Hol-lister. I may have some final truth to the man that is in this his-torical picture. His name is in fact Eddie Davenport. When he was alive we called him Murice [*sic*]. He is my wife's uncle. The things that I have read about him are some what true. The one thing that is not true is he was not a drunk. At least in his older days. He would not talk about that time in Hollister. So I can't speak about that time in his life. He did live in the Lemoore-Hanford-Tulare area in his younger days. He passed a number

of years back. He was a great man. He was very private with his life. I hope I helped with the true name and where he lived. He only has one brother left. That would be my father in law [*sic*].

Today, some motorcyclists embrace the so-called Hollister Riots as a middle finger to the establishment that, ironically, many of them—with jobs and mortgages and kids—are part of. A modern revival called the Hollister Freedom Rally gives them the chance to revel in the bad-boy image handed down to them, albeit unintentionally, by men like Eddie Davenport.

But even though the modern event is more organized and better policed, there are still occasional clashes between biker gangs, and the main drag is closed down to all vehicles except motorcycles, disrupting traffic and business. As a result the locals are still hotly divided over whether their town should celebrate the legacy of 1947 or forget it entirely.

My GPS Wants Me Dead

(CGM, 2010)

I'm not one to anthropomorphize machines. For example, I don't name my motorcycles, and I don't refer to them as "she" like sailors do with their ships. But this afternoon I broke that rule for the first time.

With my work week pretty much over, I decided this morning to go for a ride. It was shaping up to be a hot one inland, so I strapped the Camelbak onto the bike and opened all the vents on my Arai before rolling out of the garage.

I was comfortable until I had to slow down for road construction, or heavy traffic in a town; only then did I realize how hot it was. But as long as I kept moving, I was okay.

About halfway through the ride I got an urge to go to a local lake, a popular resort area with a good restaurant. I pulled over to the side of the road and searched for it on my GPS, and asked it for the shortest route.

Be careful what you wish for.

After about five miles of pavement, the road the GPS told me to take turned to graded gravel. Five more miles and the GPS told me to turn left on what appeared to be someone's driveway, but which it promised would get me to the lake in 35 minutes. That estimate didn't jive with the mileage—the lake was supposed to be just seven miles ahead—but I turned anyway.

Soon the road went from graded gravel to rough dirt, and I found out why the GPS expected it would take me more than half an hour to go seven miles. It got narrower, and rougher, and steeper, until I was feathering the clutch and picking my way up a one-lane track covered with sharp rocks the size of baseballs.

I was going so slowly the ETA on the GPS was going up, not down, as I rode. At the top of a hill that might have been a lost stage of the Dakar Rally, I stopped. Ahead of me the road dropped sharply and disappeared around a bend. The rocks were bigger and sharper than anything I'd seen so far.

I was sweating buckets by now, and not just from the walking pace I'd been riding. I was way past my comfort level, and worse, I was alone, and no one knew where I was. I turned the bike around and headed back the way I'd come.

As I said, I don't name machines, and I don't give them human attributes. But today I made an exception for my GPS, which will henceforth and forever be known as The Route Of All Evil.

Iron Butt Rally 2001

Adventure isn't fun when it's happening—oh, wait, yes it is

(RIDER, 2001)

It was a good idea, if I do say so myself. No—it was a great idea. And I blame Mike Kneebone for killing it.

Three of my buddies had signed up to ride the 2001 Iron Butt Rally—Alan Barbic, whose comprehensively rally-prepped ST1100 I wrote about when I covered the '99 IBR; Joe Zulaski, an Iron Butt rookie, aboard a similarly well-prepared ST1100; and Michael Smeyers, an IBR rookie like Zulaski but riding a K1100LT with little more in the way of rally equipment than an auxiliary fuel cell, a couple of auxiliary driving lights, and a Radio Shack timer. Three different riders, three levels of experience, and—or so I assumed—three different sets of expectations with respect to what they hoped to accomplish, and therefore three different stories in one.

Then along came Kneebone, the avuncular and twisted chairman of the Iron Butt Association, who stood up in front of 112 riders the night before the start and offered a staggering 500,000 points—the largest points value by far for a single bonus location in the history of the IBR—to any rider who could make it to Deadhorse, near Prudhoe Bay, Alaska. It was a huge ride—in Kneebone's words, "the ride of a lifetime"—and in a break with tradition, those who took a shot at the Prudhoe bonus, or the other big points-paying bonus in Alaska's Denali National Park, wouldn't have to go to any of the three regular checkpoints in California, Washington, and Maine, but were instead to return to the start/finish line in Madison, Alabama.

It was a huge roll of the dice, because in order to reach Prudhoe Bay it's necessary to ride the Dalton Highway, known to the locals as the Haul Road, 450-odd miles—one way—of gravel, mud, potholes, dirt, and desolation. Think of the worst, dustiest, muddiest, most chewed-up and rock-strewn construction zone you ever followed a pilot car through—it's Sunset Boulevard compared to the Haul Road. The weather is unpredictable, too—it can snow in August, and even a light rain turns the road to slippery mud. As if all that that weren't enough, Kneebone told the riders that once they went past the 60th parallel they were committed to Alaska. There was no going back and resuming the "normal" rally route.

And my three buddies? The ones I counted on to take different routes and make different choices based on their various backgrounds and ambitions? They all decided to shoot for Prudhoe Bay. But there's a saying among long-distance riders: "It's the ride, not the destination." To which I'll add, "No two rides are the same." No three rides, either, as it turned out, even if all three had the same destination.

Michael Smeyers had originally planned to play it safe. "Since it was my first Iron Butt Rally I wanted to ride conservatively, get to the checkpoints on time, and snag a few bonuses." In fact, such an approach, combined with normal attrition over the Rally's 11 days, is often good enough to earn a rider a middle-of-the-pack finish, nothing to scoff at in what Smeyers calls "the Olympics of long-distance motorcycling."

The Prudhoe Bay bonus wasn't really out of line with this plan. "It was less than 10,000 miles there and back," he recalls. "The weather was good right then, and if we had time on the way back we'd bag some other bonuses for insurance. It just became so clear that this was fast, do-able, and a relatively easy ride." He and his riding partner Kerry Church decided to go straight to Alaska.

Several days later, near Destruction Bay, Yukon Territory, they were separated in a construction zone. Smeyers, in the lead, suddenly realized he had lost CB contact with Church and pulled over. Fifteen minutes later he turned around and went back, only to find Church lying in a rocky ditch 10 feet below the road's surface, being tended to by a physician and an ambulance attendant.

"He was lucid and in a great deal of pain," Smeyers says. He stayed with Church right up until they loaded him in a plane and flew him to Fairbanks, Alaska. "Sending a buddy off like that is something I don't want to go through again," he says. "I'd been with him ever since 20 or 30 minutes after the wreck. Watching them put him into the plane and then fly him away, that's a terrible feeling."

Smeyers rode on to Fairbanks, checked into a room, and stayed in town for several days while Church underwent surgery on his hand and shoulder. In the meantime Smeyers's Iron Butt Rally slipped away. "I couldn't leave him there," he says. "If this had happened in Seattle or Portland or Denver, where we were a little closer to civilization, maybe my decision would have been different. But he really needed to have a familiar face around."

Joe Zulaski's reason for going to Alaska was different than Smeyers's. "I decided to go for the adventure, and screw the finish," he says. The cold didn't bother him—he had lived in Alaska for four years—but heat did, which was another point in favor of heading north. "By going to Alaska I was avoiding Texas." And like Smeyers, Zulaski thought being able to skip the regular checkpoints simplified the ride.

When he got to Fairbanks it was raining heavily, so he checked into a room and called Mike Kneebone, who was at the moment checking in riders at the Sunnyside, Washington, checkpoint. Kneebone advised sleep before making the decision whether to attempt the Haul Road. When Zulaski woke later the weather was clear and sunny. He removed all the non-essential equipment from his bike, left it in the room, and struck out for Prudhoe Bay.

In the beginning, he recalls, "it was just like hunting camp. I go hunting every year and take along trail bikes, and it was no big deal—at first. I got into some rough spots, then it smoothed out. After I crossed the Yukon River the road was chip-sealed and I was able to bring the speed up to about 50. Until then I was doing 20-25 miles an hour."

Zulaski began to regret lightening his load in Fairbanks when his front tire started to go down—one of the things he'd left behind was his tire repair kit. He was saved by a passing trucker he hailed on the CB. The trucker had a tire plug kit, but the plug, made for a truck tire, was so big they had to ream out the hole in the ST's tire to fit it.

Back on the road, things got worse. Just before Coldfoot, "the road was sort of washed out. I started going up a big hill, and that's where the mud got really bad. I'm a dirt-bike rider, and this was unlike anything I'd ever seen. I went totally sideways three different times, and I was only going 15 miles an hour. The third time I almost went off the road, and that's when I decided Denali sounded pretty good." Zulaski turned around and headed south for the easier bonus, but the going was even harder this time. "It had taken me about five hours to get to where

I was. It took me 10 full hours to get back out, because rain had turned the road behind me to mud."

Some riders would have been disappointed not to make Prudhoe Bay, but not Zulaski, who says he could have been "riding down in the hot south, sweating, looking for bonus points, longing for an air-conditioned room—Alaska was much more to my liking. It was an adventure, and the whole time, even with the flat and the mud and everything, I was having fun."

"The morning I started up the Haul Road," Alan Barbic recalls, "it was raining like crazy. I thought this is probably not a good sign. But I was committed. I decided that until the road actually shuts me down, I'm riding." The road tried its best, too, often forcing Barbic to stand on the pegs of his ST1100 for balance. "A big part of the ride was getting used to the handlebars wagging back and forth in my hands." The Alaska definition of "construction zone" took some getting used to, as well. "Sometimes the parts they had worked on were more dangerous than the parts they'd left alone."

In a construction zone north of Coldfoot, while he was waiting for the pilot car, Barbic was approached by a road worker. Standing eyeball to eyeball, the worker said, "This road is mean," and turned away. Then he turned back and added, "This road is nasty," and turned away again. His third pronouncement was, "This road is mean and nasty, and so is this place. You gotta be careful. Don't take this road for granted. Don't take your eyes off it."

After this brush with the local Welcome Wagon representative, Barbic's ride to Prudhoe was uneventful, despite some anxiety over separating from his riding partner, who had ridden on ahead. Then coming into Deadhorse his ST1100 began to misfire. Night was falling, though, so he gassed up and turned around. Then he noticed the temp gauge was pegged in the red—his radiator was caked with mud. Stripping the bodywork to get to the radiator cap, he aimed a flashlight down the filler and saw the radiator was empty.

A trucker came by just then, and offered to go for water. "A half-hour later I hear him coming back," Barbic says, "and I look and he's in reverse—he backed up the whole way from wherever he found the water." That turned out to be a tundra pond, formed by melting ice. Unable to clean the radiator, Barbic filled it and took off, stopping whenever the temperature climbed too high, riding 10 miles and stopping for 10 minutes for hours at a time.

After one cooling-off period, the bike wouldn't start up again. Off came all the bodywork again, which revealed a fuel filter clogged up solid. "You have to picture the scene," he recalls. "It's dark. There have been recent bear sightings in the area. I was told polar bears are very aggressive, like sharks. I'm not a happy camper." Working quickly if not frantically, with his bike field-stripped close to the middle of a narrow road driven mainly by large trucks, he got going again, but still had to stop every 10 miles to let the engine cool down. "Each time I got going again I thought that's 10 more miles away from the last bear that saw me."

Not even halfway back to Fairbanks, the radiator boiled dry again. Another trucker stopped, flipped on all his lights and pointed them at the bike, offered help and water, and wouldn't leave until the bike was running. Barbic eventually reached Coldfoot where he partially cured the overheating problem by pressure-washing the radiator and fabricating a mudflap out of an old tire he'd found along the way.

As a result of the Prudhoe Bay run, Barbic's bike suffered blown fork seals, oil-drenched front brakes, and broken auxiliary-tank mounts, which he replaced with rope. "That was one of the toughest rides I've ever done," he says now. Would he do it again? "In a rally, for the points, you bet. And hey, after doing that, what could be worse?"

Alan Barbie made it back to Fairbanks and from there to Madison, Alabama, where he was credited with a seventh-place finish. Joe Zulaski placed 45th. For his service to his injured comrade, Michael Smeyers was awarded the Iron Butt Medal of Valor, and a guaranteed spot in the '03 Rally. In his typically devious way, Mike Kneebone offered the Prudhoe Bay bonus again later in the Rally, after the Washington checkpoint, for a cool million points. Only one rider, Bob Hall, got there and back to Alabama in time, and was declared the winner of the 2001 Iron Butt Rally.

Beanies and Bullshit

Just one of the things
the anti-helmet guys don't want
you to know

(TREAD LIFE, 2010)

It's my own fault, really, for signing up for all those Google news alerts. A couple of the ones I get regularly are about helmets, and this evening I made the mistake of following a link to a site full of misinformation, half-truths, unsubstantiated claims, and just plain muddled thinking about helmets and why no one should be forced to wear one. And then I got my rant on.

If pinned down for an unequivocal yes or no on the issue, I'd have to say that if you don't want to wear a helmet, you shouldn't have to. I take that position for purely selfish reasons; a few of my hobbies are, shall we say, potentially hazardous to my continued health and well-being, and I don't want them to be outlawed by politicians and/or insurance companies citing the social-burden argument, which says the societal costs of an inherently dangerous activity like motorcycling (or shooting, or rock climbing, or skiing) outweigh the right of people to indulge in them.

But anti-helmet-law advocates too often take their argument a crucial step beyond the rights issue, and insist that helmets don't increase your chances of surviving a crash—in short, that they don't work. And that's where it goes off the rails.

The statistic these guys are most fond of bleating about is one that even the staunchest helmet advocates don't dispute: A motorcycle helmet isn't designed to protect you from an impact at speeds much above 13 mph. The problem with that argument is it assumes the 13 mph figure applies to the speed the bike is going when you fall off. It doesn't.

Some years ago I spoke to Dave Thom, who worked alongside the late, great Harry Hurt on the Hurt Report, which is to date still the most comprehensive, credible, and scientifically valid peer-reviewed study of the causes of motorcycle accidents. Thom knows his stuff. He's been a motorcycle-accident research assistant and associate (1977-1981), a research associate and later the laboratory director of University of Southern California's Head Protection Research Laboratory (1981-1998), and the general and senior program manager of the Head Protection Research Laboratory of Southern California (1998-2003). He's currently a senior consultant specializing in protective headgear, safety, and research at Collision and Injury Dynamics, Inc.

In short, Thom knows a lot more about helmets and motorcycle accidents than some guy from ABATE named Road Dog or Spider or Poochy.

First, I asked Thom about the 13 mph figure. "It's an important and often misunderstood point," he said. He explained that 13 mph—13.4 mph, to be precise—was the terminal velocity of an object dropped from six feet, or about the maximum height of the head of a rider seated on a motorcycle. "If you pick something up and drop it from six feet, it'll hit the ground going 13.4 mph."

But what about the speed the bike is traveling? I asked. What effect does that have on the speed at which the rider's head hits the ground?

"The speed on your speedometer is very seldom any indication of how hard you're going to hit your head," Thom said. "The only situation where it is an indication is if you hit a vertical object, like a bridge abutment. Then your speedometer speed is very important." But in most motorcycle accidents, the rider's head falls straight down and hits the ground at 13.4 mph or less. "We found way back in the Hurt studies that the typical impact on a head at the 90th percentile was *less* than the DOT impact speed of 13.4 mph."

If you need further proof that the bike's forward, or horizontal, velocity is far less important than the vertical velocity of the rider's head, said Thom, go to a motorcycle race. "If you've ever seen a guy fall off at 120, they almost always get up even though their forward speed was huge. They fall off, and they very likely hit their head at least once, but they have that six-foot fall, which is what we test helmets at."

Once you understand the bike's forward velocity is nowhere near as important as the speed at which the rider's head hits the ground, the argument that helmets don't work because they aren't designed to protect you at speeds higher than 13 mph loses virtually all of its weight.

And yet you'll see that argument put forward in most anti-helmet-law rants. The actual information is there for anyone to find, if they just look for it. But the anti-helmet faction doesn't want to look for it, and they don't want you hear about it, because it leaves them with one less bullet in their ammo belt in their fight against helmet laws.

As I said above, if you don't want to wear a helmet, don't. If you're above the age of consent, it's up to you. But there's a difference between consent and *informed* consent. Some people don't know the facts; others don't want to know them. And that's the difference between ignorance and stupidity.

The Tawdry Yet Alluring Appeal Of Riding A Beater Bike

(JALOPNIK, 2015)

When I'm looking for a new motorcycle—which is pretty much always, even when I already have a bike—I tend to buy all the motorcycle I can afford. But there are times when my budget won't stretch far enough to bring home a shiny new scoot with all the bells and farkels— times like right now, when I'm broke, bikeless, and jonesing hard for a ride.

Still, a man has needs, so this is when I pull my hat down over my eyes, turn up my collar, and head for the seedy part of the motorcycle market: Beaterville.

It's not like I'm new to that side of the tracks. At a Honda dealer where I worked for a short time, there was a loft above the service department where they stored parts that had been taken off wrecked bikes.

Most of these parts—dented gas tanks, ripped seats, a bent fork tube with a usable slider, an engine that had suffered a single broken cooling fin in an accident that completely destroyed the rest of the bike—were damaged badly enough to replace under the rider's insurance policy, but not so badly that they wouldn't work if you didn't care how they looked.

Every now and then some pimply-faced kid trying to cobble together a bike to ride to school or work would shuffle in looking for used parts. He had little or no money, which meant it wasn't a question of beating the parts department out of a sale, so someone would trudge up the stairs and dig out the dinged pipe or the bent lever that would get him on the road, accept a token donation for the Six O'Clock Beer Fund, and send him on his way before the white-shoed boss worked up the courage to see what was going on in the greasier parts of the store and came snooping around the service department.

One day the service manager was looking for something for the latest hard-luck case when he realized there was enough stuff up there to build an entire motorcycle. So he did. It was a Honda CB550K/F/WTF, with some parts from the four-pipe K model, others from the sportier F, and a few that appeared to have come from a lawnmower.

I was without a ride just then, and when he offered it to me for $600, I took it. Then as now, I was not sufficiently ruled by vanity to turn down a good deal, no matter how homely. But eventually I decided a few small cosmetic enhancements wouldn't hurt.

I put matching grips on it, found a pair of side covers the same color—though not the same color as the gas tank—and hammered out a baseball-sized divot in the front fender that rubbed on the tire. The speedometer face drooped like Dali had painted it—it's possible the instrument had been in a fire—so I found another one that looked right but had a needle that became spastic at any speed over 25 mph as if terrified of the consequences of achieving such a reckless velocity.

There was a big dent in the tank. I filled it with Bondo and spent hours sanding and refilling it to a contour that stubbornly refused to match that of the surrounding metal, dispelling any illusions that I might have had about a fallback career as a body-and-fender man. I painted the tank in what turned out to be the ugliest shade of orange ever—the color on the can was probably listed as Ugly Orange. The resulting finish had the same texture as the peel of an orange, though, so in the end it was an inspired choice.

I don't remember how many miles I put on that bike, mainly because I don't remember how many speedometers from the loft I put on it until I found one that worked for more than a week. I remember one odd trait it had—the quietest idle of any bike I'd ridden before or since. Most of the time, if it hadn't been for the tach needle twitching like a frog leg hooked up to a car battery, I wouldn't have known the engine was running at all.

Compared to the bikes I'd owned before, including a snarling Ducati and a spotless Yamaha triple I bought from a concours judge, the CB550 represented several dozen rungs down on the prestige ladder. At first I wanted to wear a helmet with someone else's name on it so nobody would recognize me, but it wasn't long before I discovered the tawdry yet alluring appeal of riding a beater.

A beater proved to be the perfect excuse on weekend rides. If I got to the lunch spot first, the other guys would say, "Wow, he goes pretty fast on that old beater!" and if I was last they'd say, "Well, of course he's slow, look at that old beater he's riding." If someone else's newer bike crapped out and had to be fetched home in a borrowed pickup, he caught shit because mine didn't. If it was mine in the back of the truck, nobody was surprised.

Despite having one of my previous bikes stolen, I didn't worry about the CB550, which looked as appetizing as the rejected produce in the Dumpster behind a Safeway. It was so ugly no one would want to steal it, and even if someone had boosted it, the other bike thieves would have made fun of him until he brought it back.

In 1984 I was offered a job at *Rider*, which required moving from the Bay Area to L.A. Since I'd have access to new and infinitely nicer-looking bikes in my capacity as features editor, I sold the CB550 to a friend of a friend before I left, for the same $600 I'd paid for it.

If I could find another like it today I'd snap it up in a heartbeat. But all the CB550s I find on Craigslist are non-running junk, or have been café'd, bobbered—which is to say irrevocably rat-fucked—or meticulously restored right out of my price range. I'm not into cruisers, as they just don't do what I want a motorcycle to do, and all I have to do is look at a dual-sport and I can taste rocks and dirt and loose teeth.

I see more beater sportbikes for sale than anything else. There's something about the lure of speed mixed with the heedlessness of youth that turns many a fine high-performance motorcycle into a rolling trash heap that looks like it was dragged behind a truck through a quarry. I avoid the big-bore sufferers of this affliction because if you need to replace or repair anything major it's going to cost you big.

At the other end of the price scale are used and used-up Ninja 250s. They're as plentiful as fleas on a stray dog, and tempting if only to bring back memories of the high-revving two-strokes I started riding and racing on. But I'm a big guy, and they're so small I'd need one for each foot, like skates. Lately, though, there's a Ninja 650R I have my eye on, and it might be my next cheap date.

My friend Larry has ridden it from his home in Oregon to Alaska, Nova Scotia, and Mexico, and it bears the scars of Dempster chip-seal pavement, the petrified remains of every insect species between the Pacific Coast and the Maritimes, and evidence of the hard-knock life of a middleweight twin drafted into pack-mule touring duty.

You could look all day and not find a square foot of bodywork without a scratch, a crack, or a hole inflicted by road debris somewhere in North America. But even though the valves haven't been checked in 36,000 miles—since new, in fact—the engine still ticks over like a Swiss watch, and runs smoke-free and oil-dry. It even has new tires and a Scottoiler.

The Ninja was the darling of Larry's fleet, but lately it's just another toy to push around the garage so he can get at one of his seven (or is it eight?) other bikes. He's thinking it's time the Ninja went away, and I'm thinking "away" should be my garage. I figure a couple of weeks of after-dinner wrench sessions and a jumbo helping of sweat equity can get this little darlin' looking pretty good.

Guys on newer bikes will still park down the street to avoid looking like they're riding with me, but I'll just smile and wave as I ride past the Beaterville city limits sign and out into the world of cheap fun.

What I Learned
Riding 1000 Miles On A
Motorcycle In 24 Hours

(JALOPNIK, 2015)

When I first heard about an under-the-radar bunch of road riders who rode 1000 miles in 24 hours or less just to earn membership in something called the Iron Butt Association, I thought, *A thousand miles? In one day? That's what airplanes are for. What's wrong with these guys?* So I decided to find out.

This was in July 2000, and by then I'd been riding motorcycles for 32 years, some of which were spent roadracing at the club and pro level. In the late 1980s I was on staff at three motorcycle magazines, where the garage full of test bikes was referred to as "the candy store," and on any given day I could ride a cruiser, a tourer, a sportbike, or a dual-sport. Motorcycles were both my profession and my preferred method of travel, and I fancied myself a tough, experienced rider.

But even to me, what the Iron Butt Association was doing seemed a bit extreme. The group says it's "dedicated to safe, long-distance motorcycle riding," an endeavor some see as the most boring way possible to turn gasoline into smog and others see as recklessly irresponsible.

After all, what's "safe" about running flat out for 1000 miles on public roads, endangering buses full of nuns, and startling soccer moms texting their friends about little Chad Jr.'s game-winning goal?

The first thing I learned is you don't need to run flat out, nor do you really want to. Riding fast means higher gas consumption and more gas stops; more frequent stops to rest; and the increased likelihood of roadside conversations with local law-enforcement personnel. The clock is ticking the whole time.

Then I did the math. A thousand miles in 24 hours is a 42 mph average. Not even my mom would call that a reckless pace, and she hated motorcycles, referring to them until her dying day as "those things." Even with stops for gas, food, and calls of nature, I figured could leave early, spend the entire ride on the Interstate, and be back home in time to catch Letterman.

OK, but what about the bike? You need a big touring rig, right, or a fast sportbike? Negatory, good buddy. Any two-wheeled conveyance that's comfortable, has decent range, and is capable of keeping up with freeway traffic will do the job. Riders have done their Saddlesore 1000, a.k.a. SS1K, on scooters, fer cryin' out loud. Your Bonneville or SV650 will be fine.

At the time I decided to see what this craziness was all about, I was a contributing editor to a Harley magazine (remember magazines?) called *American Rider*, which has long since succumbed to the fate that all print magazines seem destined for. There was a dark green Heritage Softail in my garage, on loan from the press pool at H-D's fleet center.

With floorboards, a custom seat, and a rider backrest, it was like sitting in a fast, loud recliner. It had a barn-door windscreen and a pair of fringed, faux-leather saddlebags that wouldn't have looked out of place on a cow pony. I put maps, some tools, a heated vest, some granola bars, and a few bottles of water in them, and with a planned departure of 4 a.m., hit the sack.

When I rolled into the Chevron station the next morning to fill the tank, neither I nor the pump jockey seemed as awake as we'd have liked. I asked him to witness the mileage on the odometer, and confirm my starting time. Using witness forms at the start and end of the ride, and the time-stamped and dated gas receipts I got along the way, the IBA could confirm I'd actually done the ride—you can't just say, "Yeah, I rode 1000 miles in 24 hours, now gimme my membership card." (There aren't membership cards anyway; you get a certificate and a license-plate backer.) With the starting documentation and the first gas receipt in the saddlebag I hit the road.

I started in Coos Bay, Oregon, where I lived at the time. From there I'd ride east on Highway 42 to I-5, north to Portland, around Portland on I-205, to I-84 to La Grande, Oregon—a little over 500 miles—then turn around and come home the same way. Boring? Maybe. Efficient? Absolutely.

Like a lot of riders whose posts I'd read on Internet forums, I was pretty wound up for the first hundred miles or so, giddy from the scope of what I was attempting—A thousand miles! In one day!—but the ride quickly resolved itself into… just another ride.

I hit some rain around dawn, and again a few hours later. My Acrostich Darien jacket and pants shed water like a Cordura-nylon duck's ass so I didn't have to stop to put on raingear. The sun came out and I took off my heated vest at a gas station. I'd read about how much time some riders wasted at gas stops and had practiced getting mine under three minutes from engine off to engine on, a challenge in no-self-serve Oregon.

The Heritage gobbled the miles, the Twin Cam B engine churning out torque like water pouring from a bucket. Cruising at 70 was effortless, and by the time I looped around Portland and headed east along the Columbia River I was having such a good time that if I'd had to stop and turn around right then I'd have counted it a damn fine day of riding.

I stopped for a short rest in The Dalles, napping leaned up against a low wall beside a gas station, known in the long-distance riding community as "checking in to the Iron Butt Motel." A couple of granola bars on waking, and a bottle of water, and it was on to La Grande, Oregon, the town I'd picked as my turnaround point because it was 500 miles—plus a few for insurance—from my point of departure.

I got another gas receipt, turned the Heritage around, and headed for the barn. Some people I'd talked to said they couldn't see the point of riding through all that pretty country without stopping to see any of it. But I saw more in a day than most riders see in a week. The broad Columbia, rolling through the withered brown hills around Boardman. Windsurfers near The Dalles, jumping frothy waves the stiff wind kicked up on the river. Controlled field fires lofting towering columns of smoke into the blue sky. Multnomah Falls, gushing from a cleft in the green cliffs. I didn't stop for any of them, but I'll never forget them.

South of Portland, with the sun going down, I started to feel pressured to speed it up. I needn't have. Traffic bowled along at 75, and I exited I-5 late that night with less than 100 miles to go and more than four hours to do it. Not wanting to be the guy who crashes on the last lap while comfortably in the lead, I stopped for coffee twice, and backed off my pace through prime deer country.

It was dark when I pulled into the Coos Bay Chevron station to get my finishing receipt and asked the same pump jockey to certify my ending mileage and sign the witness form. I'd covered 1073 miles in a little under 22 hours, and I hadn't died, not even once.

So, what did I get out of spending almost an entire day droning along on the Interstate, other than a certificate, a license-plate backer that proclaimed I was one of the "World's Toughest Riders!" (a blatant falsehood in my case), a saddlebag full of memories that will still be with me when I'm too old to swing a leg over a bike, and a genuine respect and admiration for the Heritage Softail?

In that short ride I learned skills that I still use today. I don't speed—much—and I still get where I'm going on time. If I need to, I can cover a lot of ground on a bike at a good clip without getting tired. Riding a Saddlesore taught me to focus on the long haul, and that staying in the saddle at a consistent pace beats the hell out of going flat out until I drop or get stopped. And maybe best of all, it boosted my self-confidence and broadened my horizons to include a world of motorcycling I never knew existed.

Also, now I know what's wrong with these guys: They let me into their club. (I should have warned them...) At least I'm not alone. Today there are over 60,000 IBA members, and every one of them rode at least a Saddlesore to get in—there are many other certificate rides, most harder than the SS1K, and a few that seem like the invention of a sadist.

I made a lot of very good friends through the IBA, and though some of them are genuinely crazy, it's a really good kind of crazy.

It'll take you just 24 hours or less to add your own kind of crazy to the mix.

Of Mice And Muck

(TREAD LIFE, 2009)

During the time I worked at *Cycle Guide*, my then partner, Mary, worked in the art department of *Road & Track*. *R&T* and *Cycle World* were in the same building, and Peter Egan wrote for both titles, so he and Mary sometimes worked together.

One year Egan bought a new toolbox, and Mary bought his old one and gave it to me as a birthday present. Because she knew I admired his writing, she got him to scratch his autograph in the paint under the lid.

I brought the toolbox with me when we moved to Oregon in 1988. After a couple of years in a house in town, I bought a three-and-a-half-acre property outside of town, which we shared with two dogs, some deer, the occasional owl, and a million small rodents.

About a dozen of those rodents took up residence in the toolbox, which lived in the unfinished half of the basement. I discovered this one day when I pulled open a drawer looking for a 5mm hex key, and instead found a clump of dryer lint with a depression in the middle big enough for several generations of mice to snooze in. The drawer under that one was stuffed to capacity with another nest. The bottom drawer was carpeted with mouse crap.

I cleaned out the toolbox and a month later they were back. The smell was horrific, and eventually I left the squatters in possession of their home and moved my tools elsewhere, fully intending to get in there someday and reclaim it for its intended use.

I never got around to it, until tonight. I'm in a new house now, and for the first time in more than 20 years I have an enclosed garage where I can work on bikes in comfort, and by golly, I want my toolbox back. So I removed the drawers, held my nose while I pried out the urine- and crap-soaked felt pads lining each one, and took the drawers outside where I sprayed them with S-100 and then hosed them down.

After taking the drawers out I found several things that had fallen down behind them. I found a 10mm wrench I thought I'd lost years ago. I found a receipt from a Snap-on dealer for a tool of some kind sold to "Elroy's" sometime in the 1960s. (Note to self: Ask Egan about this sometime.) I also found out that dried mouse pee smells just as bad almost 20 years later as it did the day it passed through the mouse—bad enough to make my eyes water. I might have to burn the clothes I was wearing.

This job might take a while. Hell, it might take a hazmat team.

Pilgrimage

(TREAD LIFE, 2009)

I received an email this afternoon from the editor of *Rider* about an article I sold him last year, a touring story about a ride down to Sonoma, California, for Harley's 2009 model intro. He had just now gotten around to reading it in preparation for running it in the next issue, and mentioned that he liked it—"Great story!"

Distant as I am from the nuts and bolts of magazine production, I don't typically get much feedback about my work. I write a piece, I email it to the editor, and a check arrives at some indeterminate point in the future, by which time I've long since moved on to the next assignment. So when the email arrived today, I searched the story on the computer and punched up the Sonoma piece, curious to see what made it stand out.

I still don't know, because I got to a certain point in the piece and was stopped cold by a rush of memory:

On the way back through San Francisco I stopped at the Golden Gate Recreation Area north of the bridge and climbed the winding road until I found a place to pull over that was more or less free of tourists. As I do every time I pass this way, I stood a while looking out at the city where I was born. It's a beautiful, almost magical place, and, perched as it is on the San Andreas Fault, maybe a doomed place, as well. That's why I make this pilgrimage to the high cliffs above it every chance I get.

Although I was born in San Francisco, I lived there only for three days before I was taken across the bay to an orphanage in Oakland, where I was adopted by my parents. It's fashionable these days to differentiate adoptive parents from biological parents, but I never did, and I still don't. They were my parents. End of discussion.

In 1973 I moved to Marin County, just north of San Francisco, and it was from there that many of the misadventures of my motorcycling youth were launched. I got a job as an apprentice machinist at an aftermarket motorcycle accessory distributor and manufacturer, and lived for a month in my dad's camper pick-up in the parking lot, driving it home to Santa Clara on the weekends, until I found an apartment in San Rafael.

The apartment had no garage—it barely had walls—so I stowed my Honda CB500 Four street bike and my TZ250 roadracer in the back of my employer's warehouse. I became a regular on the Sunday Morning Ride, an appallingly dangerous and occasionally deadly street ride/ outlaw race/lemming march up Highway 1, where—to shamelessly rip off one of Jeff Karr's most memorable lines—I saw Jesus so many times I started using him as a brake marker.

Life on two wheels was very different back then. After the Honda, I rode a 900cc Ducati Darmah SS, dressed in jeans, Full Bore roadracing boots, and a Bell Helmets down jacket that would have evaporated in a red puff of nylon dust had I crashed in it. I was particularly proud of the buckskin gardening gloves I had bought at Orchard Supply Hardware for 14 bucks a pair. Helluva deal.

I continued to ride south to visit my parents every weekend, taking Highway 101 over the Golden Gate, through the City on 19th Avenue, and on to Highway 280. In summer the ride was spectacular, thanks to a dense gray tunnel of fog that barreled in from the ocean, blanketed the towers of the bridge, and rolled across the bay until it broke apart on the Oakland hills. Pouring through the Golden Gate, hunkered down on the water like an enormous slug, it looked like a blind, remorseless, world-swallowing monster in a Norse myth.

It was cold, too. I'd start out in Marin in light gear and be shivering and damp by the time I got to Golden Gate Park. A few miles later the fog vanished, and the bright sun beat down on me again, turning the cold dampness to sticky sweat.

In the folly that was my youth, I never took the time to wander around San Francisco much. I was too eager to get somewhere else, and had no appreciation of where I already was. I didn't feel any real connection with the city then, except the accident of my birth there.

It was only later on, after moving to Oregon, that I started feeling that odd tug that seems to pull some people back to their place of origin. And so began the ritual of never passing through San Francisco without pausing to ride up the narrow road on the north side of the bridge to look down on the shining city by the bay.

A while ago, before I sat down to write this, I went out to the backyard to play fetch with Daisy, Tread Life's editorial assistant and morale officer. Daisy's version of fetch involves a lot of chewing the ball, and rolling around on it, and sniffing the spot where she rolled, so I bring my iPod along to fill the interludes between throws.

As I scrolled down the playlists I came to Van Morrison's *Astral*

Weeks, an album that got a lot of airplay during my time in Marin, and has since become for me a touchstone of those years. I clicked on the title track, and just as the guitar started strumming, a cool breeze out of the south swept over the backyard fence, bringing with it a whiff of what I could have sworn was salty air, with a hint of cool, damp fog, and before I knew it I was standing at the edge of a cliff overlooking a brick-red bridge, its towers framing a shining white city in the distance.

Rhymes With Crazy

(TREAD LIFE, 2009)

I'm not an entirely happy camper lately. My back has been giving me hell, and I haven't been riding much because of it. But there's
someone in the house who's not bothered by this, and that's Tread Life's
editorial assistant and morale officer, Daisy.

I got Daisy nine years ago from the local animal shelter. I'd been
looking for a buddy for my Golden Retriever, Winzer, and stopped by
the shelter to see if there were any likely candidates.

I walked down the row of pens containing dogs that were either
barking loudly enough to deafen a rock, or cowering in the corner as far
as possible from strangers like me. Daisy was different. She sat silently
by the door of the pen, her tail twitching tentatively, looking sad and
scared, and yet a bit hopeful.

I leaned down for a closer look, and saw her left ear had a wad of
what appeared to be Scotch tape on it, holding together a ragged tear in
the tip of the ear about an inch long. Some sort of goo had been slopped

on the car before the tape was applied. It looked like first aid applied by an office temp. It's a good thing there hadn't been a stapler handy.

The shelter worker told me that was the way she'd been found. No one knew how old she was, but they guessed about six months. She looked for all the world like a very young Golden Retriever, the exact same color as Winzer, and with the same hair, of the same length, in all the same places.

But I wasn't ready to take anyone home that day, so I left. Next time I drove by the shelter I stopped in again, and Daisy was still there. It struck me as odd that no one had taken her yet. She was apparently well behaved, and as cute as a dog gets.

I remarked on this to the shelter worker. She couldn't understand it, either. It was a shame, too, she said, because Daisy had been there a while, and if no one took her home in the next week or so her next stop was the small room out back, where dogs go in but don't come out.

I think at that point I might have been ready to take her home, but I left and went home to think about it some more. Adding another dog to the family was a big deal. Would she and Winzer get along? Would I have the time to train her like I'd trained Winzer? Could I afford to feed and pay the vet bills on two dogs? (Money was tight back then, but when isn't it?)

It wasn't long before I decided everything would work out somehow. That, and the thought of her getting the needle made up my mind. I picked up Daisy at the shelter, paid the adoption fee, and took her— torn ear and all—straight to my vet, who pronounced her healthy and gave her a series of shots; there was no way of telling when or if she'd had shots last, but there was no harm in repeating them.

It was while we were sitting in the vet's waiting room as the paperwork was being filled out that Daisy got her name. The rabies certificate had a space on it for the dog's name. At that point I hadn't picked one out yet, figuring I'd let her tell me what she should be named in her own time.

But bureaucracy would not be denied—no name, no rabies certificate. The other people in the waiting room began suggesting names. Most of them made me want to puke. Then I thought about the comic strip "Blondie," and the dog in it. The dog at my feet looked just like that dog.

"Daisy," I said. "Her name is Daisy."

As I said, that was nine years ago. Since then, several things have become apparent. First, Daisy is part Golden Retriever and part something else, maybe Border Collie—which would account for her size—but certainly something high-drive and obsessive. (Although I could be wrong about that. I've since learned Golden Retrievers come not only in several colors, from almost white to rusty red, but they vary greatly in size, too. High drive and obsessive behavior are not uncommon, either.)

Second, she is a very smart dog. I haven't trained her to the level I did Winzer, who earned an AKC CD title and one leg of his CDX before both of us got tired of the fussy precision of the sport and hung it up in favor of getting good at chasing tennis balls. But Daisy does all the things a well-behaved dog needs to do—sits, stays, comes when she's called—and does them willingly.

And third, she's a lot happier when I don't spend hours riding a motorcycle, but instead hang around the house throwing things for her to bring back so I can throw them again.

I have to admit I kind of like it, too. Winzer passed last year, leaving Daisy an only dog. Since then, free of the anxiety of having to share my attention, she's become a calmer, more mature dog, who no longer tries to run away or digs under fences, and who heels nicely on a slack leash, and likes to go with me to the coffee shop and sit at a table outside and lean against my leg, sniffing the breeze.

So although I'm not happy about not riding, it's not as bad as it could be. Daisy has been keeping me amused. But even she has to sleep sometime—she's napping on the floor behind me as I write this—and while she's dozing I'm wondering just how she'd like riding in a sidecar.

Because I have to believe that if riding motorcycles is as much fun as it is, and dogs are as much fun as they are, how much more fun would the two of them together be?

The Franco Files

1987 Yamaha new model intro

(TREAD LIFE, 2010)

In November of 1986 *Cycle Guide* editor Jim Miller tapped me to go to France in early December to cover Yamaha's 1987 new-model into. I'd never been out of the country up until then, nor had I ever been on the cover of *CG*. I'd be doing both very soon.

Some highlights of that trip follow.

Our flight began in Los Angeles and ended in Marseilles after about 20 hours in the air and in various airports. When we got to the hotel in the seaside town of Bandol, it was early morning local time, and who-the-hell-knows internal-clock time. Several of us wandered around the wakening town in a daze looking for something to eat, and found a vendor selling roast-beef sandwiches out of a cart by the waterfront.

As I ate my sandwich I noticed an odd scent on the breeze. It was warm, heavy, totally unfamiliar and familiar at the same time. It seemed to be coming from the south. I looked that way and realized where it was coming from. Africa.

Africa. Right over *there*, across that short stretch of water. I was so struck with how far from home I was that I wouldn't be surprised if my jaw actually dropped.

I scrambled down a rocky slope to the beach and dipped my hand in the water of the Mediterranean and thought about all the history that had taken place on the shores of that sea. Greece. Egypt. Rome. I'd never been out of the U.S. before, and look where I was.

Suddenly there was a huge splash next to me. My jet-lagged colleagues were pitching rocks at me, and laughing like madmen.

And just like that, it was as if I'd never left home.

We were sitting around a table at an outdoor café in some small town, talking about the old stone houses that lined the narrow cobbled street. Someone asked the French Sonauto rep how old they were, and he said, "Oh, many of them are very old." One of the U.S. journos said he was from back east, where some of the house were 400 years old. The Sonauto rep laughed and said, "Here, the *new* houses are 400 years old."

We had dinner one night in a restaurant in Bandol. While we ate, a guitar player, maybe 17 years old, strummed away on a stool by the door. One of the journos thought it would be funny to get the kid drunk, and sent glass after glass of wine over to him. The kid had probably started drinking wine with his meals when he was seven, and just smiled and thanked the journo with each glass. By the time we left, the kid's playing was still flawless, which was more than could be said for the journo's walking.

There was a sign on the wall of the Paris airport where we changed planes. It said, "Luggage left unattended will be instantly destroyed by the police." As if to hammer the point home, there was no lost and found in the airport terminal.

At a lunch stop lunch in Cannes, I was seated next to one of the French National Police officers assigned to escort us. He was wearing a stainless-steel revolver in a white leather holster. I asked him what type of gun it was, and to my surprise he pulled it out of the holster, popped open the cylinder, dumped the rounds on the table, and handed it to me. If I'd had any doubt that I was no longer in America, that dispelled it.

The Mistral straight at Circuit Paul Ricard was about a mile long. I was about two-thirds of the way to the end of it when I glanced down at the speedo of the FZR1000 I was riding and saw the needle swing past the 165 mph mark. Corrected for speedometer error, that was close to 160 actual. That's the fastest I've ever gone on a motorcycle, and the fastest I ever care to. Since it had been only five months since I'd had a big crash at Willow Springs that took me several months to recover from, I decided it was also as fast as I needed to go for the rest of the trip. I came into the pits and handed the FZR over to someone else.

Near the end of a banzai street ride from Bandol to Monaco, we stopped at a turnout overlooking the harbor of Monte Carlo. We could see almost the entire country from up there. I tried to pick out the streets that made up the track the Formula 1 cars ran on. Clem Salvadori was standing nearby, and since he spoke French I asked him to ask our French National Police escort to point it out.

They did better than that. After we crossed the border into Monaco, they led us on a couple of laps of the course, motioning slow cars out of the way so we could wick it up some on the straight bits. *Do they have jurisdiction here?* I wondered. I still don't know. But I wasn't complaining.

During an off-day in Monte Carlo a few of us went to Le Roche de Monaco (the Rock of Monaco), site of the palace of Prince Albert. We found a small restaurant nearby and went inside for lunch. One of us spoke a bit of high-school French and tried to order for everyone. The waitress waited patiently while he savaged her native tongue without managing to put together a coherent sentence. Finally she said, "Pizza for four and a pitcher of beer, is that right?" in near-perfect English. We would run into this phenomenon—French speakers who were reluctant or too embarrassed or contrary to speak English—several times during the trip.

On our last night in Monaco we had a huge dinner in the hotel restaurant and later walked to a nearby casino. We handed over our passports at the door and were directed to a cavernous room that was half empty. At the far end were some gaming tables and slot machines.

I'm not a gambler, but I have no objection to watching other people gamble. A few of the journos sat down at a baccarat table and lost quite a lot of what they would later realize was not expense money, but their own money, since the casino didn't give receipts for gambling losses, and their magazines' accounting departments weren't about to reimburse them for doubling down on a bad hand.

We were doing just fine there for a while, enriching the local economy, when somebody spilled a drink. On the felt baccarat table. In the middle of a hand. We were asked to remove ourselves, given back our passports, and shown the door.

Before the trip we had all been sent an information sheet by Yamaha outlining the itinerary, the travel schedules, and what to bring, including attire suitable for formal occasions, which is to say a suit and a tie, not just a spare clean T-shirt.

I bought a suit, but I ran out of time and money before I found a pair of dress shoes. Which is how I ended up as the only guest in a luxurious five-star hotel to be seated at a lavish six-course dinner wearing new, shiny black Bates roadracing boots.

A week after I got back to the office I filled out my expense report and turned it in. The next day the money guy walked up to my desk and tossed a small piece of paper on it. It was a 30-franc receipt from the

Oceanographical Museum of Monaco, where I had spent a few hours looking at bizarre sea creatures in jars of formaldehyde.

"Your souvenir receipt got mixed up with the real ones," he said, and went back to his office.

Hey, you can't blame a guy for trying.

The Longest Ride

The true meaning of the buddy system

(RIDER)

It's hard to find a good riding buddy. It's even harder to lose one.

Dick Fish and Jim Young became friends after a long-distance rally in Utah in 2000. Young, with his traditional post-rally cigar, was riding his bike up the loading ramp into the back of his truck when he lost his balance. He and the bike fell over, and he ended up with a windscreen upright piercing his arm and pinning him to the ground. Fish was one of the riders who rushed to his aid, and later took him to the hospital, where the two began to form a close bond.

Young was a career Army officer, a Ranger and West Point graduate with 27 years of service and four master's degrees. He worked with Apache helicopter weapons systems and attained the rank of colonel before he retired. He was leading a semi-nomadic life when he and Fish met, living out of his truck and getting in as much riding as possible. He knew he'd have to go back to work soon to help put his kids through college, but until then he was determined to see as much of the world on two wheels as he could.

Fish and Young became riding buddies, and began competing in long-distance rallies as a team. In such rallies the idea is to ride against the clock to far-flung bonus locations worth varying points. The trick is juggling the distances, the available time, and the value of each bonus to allow time for sleep and refueling on the way. Each rider had strengths the other lacked. Fish could ride farther and longer than Young, but Young's strategic skills made sure they got the most points for the miles they rode. "I could outride Jim, but he could out-think me," Fish says. "We were a great pair that way."

One rally they didn't ride together—Fish had other commitments that prevented it—turned out to be Jim Young's last. In 2001, he went off the road on Colorado 90, about nine miles from the Utah border at a place called Paradox Hill. Bike and rider slid down a steep cliff and came to rest in the underbrush. Young likely died instantly. It took search crews and fellow rally riders six days to find him.

Fish was devastated by the loss of his friend. He acquired the wrecked bike with the intent of rebuilding it as a tribute to his riding partner, and at the same time began planning a ride in his honor, as well. "Jim had always wanted to do a big North American ride," Fish says, "something that nobody else had done. I had it in my mind to get his bike, but I didn't put that together with doing this ride until a couple of months before."

The ride that Fish envisioned was certainly one nobody else had done before. His goal was nothing less than to ride just about as far north, south, east, and west as possible on the North American continent. His ride, which he called the Jim Young Memorial Ride, would take him to Goose Bay, Labrador; Key West, Florida; Cabo San Lucas, Mexico; Paradox Hill, Colorado; and Prudhoe Bay, Alaska. His goal was to complete the ride in under 20 days, and do it on Jim Young's bike.

The route presented enormous strategic difficulties beyond just riding the miles. "To do this ride," Fish says, "you really have to think about the fact that you're doing Prudhoe, where it can snow any day of the year, and you're doing Mexico, so if you wait until Prudhoe is ideal in terms of warmth, you're looking at 120 degrees in the south." Fish had wanted to get the unpredictable run up the Haul Road to Prudhoe Bay and back out of the way first, but the weather there didn't look good. So on July 3 he decided he'd deal with whatever the Haul Road had in store for him later, and instead headed east from his home in Cardston, Alberta, to Goose Bay.

Labrador is wild and rocky and sparsely inhabited. It's said that when God finished making the world, he took what was left over and made Labrador. Fish rode to Baie Comeau, Quebec, and went north to the Labrador Highway. About 130 miles later, near a power station called Manic 5, the pavement stopped. The road was dirt the rest of the way to Goose Bay—wet, too, recalls Fish. "It rained all the time I was on the Labrador Highway," he says.

Fish reached Goose Bay, documented his arrival and took a photo, and headed back out the way he'd come in. After the severe conditions on the Labrador Highway, the all-interstate run down the east coast to Key West, Florida, must have seemed like a walk in the park.

From Key West, Fish pointed his wheels toward Cabo San Lucas, Mexico. His plan was to catch the ferry at Topolobampo, take it across the Gulf of California to La Paz, and then ride to Cabo. But he had to get to Topolobampo first. "That was he toughest day, and the day that I thought I wasn't going to make it. I rode from Fort Stockton, Texas, to Topolobampo. I had a four-hour cushion to make that ferry, and if

I missed it there wasn't another one for two days. I got there with 45 minutes to spare."

Not only was time against him, so, it seems were the Mexican roads, one of which gave him the only scary moment in the entire ride. "I came around a corner and hit some gravel and lost the front end. I've never been so close to high-siding in my life without actually doing it. To this day I don't know how I stayed on it."

From Cabo San Lucas Fish headed north to his next stop, the site of Jim Young's crash near Paradox Hill in Colorado. But getting out of Mexico proved much harder than getting in. "You have to have paperwork for your motorcycle as well as yourself if you're going more than 50 miles into Mexico," Fish says. "The problem is you have to hand this paperwork in when you leave. The office in Tecate, a small crossing, wasn't open. There's a tiny border crossing on the west side of Yuma, Arizona, but that crossing couldn't accept the paperwork. I had to go to San Luis Colorado."

On the way there he rode by a bank sign that displayed a temperature of 118 degrees. At last he rid himself of the troublesome paperwork and made for the U.S. border—along with thousands of other travelers. "It took me two hours from the time I got to San Luis Colorado to the time I got back into the U.S."

After his stop at Paradox Hill Fish continued on to his house in Cardston, where he spent four hours changing the oil and putting a fresh rear tire on the bike. The last leg of his journey lay ahead, north to Alaska and up the Haul Road to Prudhoe Bay.

The Haul Road starts where the pavement ends, not far north of Fairbanks. Some people would say civilization ends there, too. The weather and the road surface are unpredictable, and services are non-existent except at a few remote places like Coldfoot, about halfway between Fairbanks and Prudhoe Bay. "I got to Coldfoot at 8:42 p.m.,"

Fish recalls. "That time of year it was continuous daylight—the sun never totally sets. I was still feeling good, and it was too early to stop. So I went for Prudhoe. It might have been a mistake, though, because the sun was right on the road—it had just gone down, touched the horizon, and stayed right there, right in my face. Every time I went up a little hill I was totally blind. It stayed that way the whole way."

Fish pulled into Deadhorse, the last town before Prudhoe Bay and the end of the road for non-employees of the oil fields, at 1:15 in the morning on July 18, 2003, in full daylight. There were two hotels, both offering tiny rooms for $125 a night. Fish checked into one for about six hours of sleep, rode back to Fairbanks through temperatures in the high 20s, crossed the Yukon Territories into British Columbia, riding through desolate places with names like Destruction Bay and Prophet River, and pulled into his driveway in Cardston two days later, almost three days ahead of schedule.

Jim Young had many friends in motorcycling, and Fish credits several of them with helping him prepare the bike for the ride. Bill "Rocky" Mayer donated a seat, and Tim Bernard of Happy Trails supplied parts and accessories—"probably the biggest help financially," says Fish. Mark Reis did a lot of the original accessory wiring on Young's bike, and re-did it all for Fish's ride. And Paige Ortiz of Aeroflow came through with discounted parts.

Even with all the help, Fish says the Jim Young Memorial Ride "was one of the toughest things I've ever done in my life." It was made even tougher by the absence of his friend and riding buddy. But you can bet Jim was there, looking over Fish's shoulder, every mile of the way, smoking one of his big cigars.

(Dick Fish lost his life in a traffic accident in 2011 while riding through Glacier National Park in Montana.)

Ferry Tales

(TREAD LIFE, 2009)

Relaxing is hard work. This evening, belatedly realizing how low my energy tank had been drained by my Canadian sojourn, and unrefreshed by an hour-long nap midday, I succumbed to the inevitable and took to my bed at about 5 p.m. It's now 9:30 p.m., and thanks to that peculiar filtering process that enables writers unconsciously to distill their thoughts into a semi-coherent whole before committing them to paper, I feel up to jotting down some notes about the trip for those who haven't already turned up their noses because I drove my car instead of riding my bike.

A word about that first. "To travel is better than to arrive" is a sentiment I've never fully accepted. I guess that makes me some sort of philistine, but the truth is most journeys bore me. I travel in order to arrive, and the way I look at it, the less time the traveling takes, the more time I have to enjoy the place I'm traveling to. The only reason some people remember so much about how they got to where they were going is that it took so damn long to get there. Mark my words—if they ever develop a practical *Star Trek*-type transporter, I won't be the only one using it.

All that said, there is one form of travel—necessarily slow, and a bit complicated, and fairly expensive on a dollar-per-mile basis—that I find absolutely charming, and that's ferries. British Columbia has an excellent ferry system, imaginatively named B.C. Ferries, that is the primary carrier between Vancouver Island and mainland Canada, and across a couple of bays on the western shore of B.C., which is called the Sunshine Coast. There are also ferries that run farther up the west coast, and I plan to take them one day.

I rode two ferries on this trip. The first took me (and the car) from Port Angeles, Washington, over to Victoria on Vancouver Island, and reacquainted me with the reason why I'll never make a good sailor. The rain had been bucketing down for most of the previous day; in the morning it was windy as we left the dock, and once truly under way, the waves got choppy, as well. To look at the ferry from afar you wouldn't guess something of that size could be tossed around that much, but I swear there were times when we were headed in three directions at once. I won't say the sight of other passengers eating breakfast made mine want to come up, but I had a few moments there when the deck seemed a better place to be than inside the cabin.

Victoria, the largest city on Vancouver Island, and the capital of the province of British Columbia, has been called a city of "newlyweds, nearly deads, and flower beds," which neatly encompasses its reputation as a holiday destination, its high percentage of resident retirees, and its beautiful gardens, including the famous Butchart Gardens. The British influence is evident everywhere, enhanced by a constant parade of people of all ethnic and national backgrounds. For reasons I can't fathom, I felt instantly at home there.

I spent two days in Saanich, north of Victoria, at a Howard Johnson motel staffed by individuals hell-bent on living up to the rest of the world's notion that Canadians are excessively polite people. Even the local buses were apologetic ("Sorry, I am not in service"). I walked around Victoria far more than was good for my weak ankle, and reflected on the idea that had I come here on a bike, I'd be chafing to get back on it and go looking for good roads. But the road wasn't why I was here; it was where the road took me that mattered.

On my third day in Canada I drove to Nanaimo, on the east coast of the island, home to the ferry that would take me to the mainland the next day. Nanaimo has a neat little downtown, full of cafes and pubs and artsy shops and—here I bare my geekiness to you, gentle readers—used-book stores, which I dearly love to browse through. Leafing through an obscure volume that hasn't seen the light of day for years, or a forgotten copy of a book I love, with the musty smell of old paper and cracked binding glue wafting up from the pages, does for me what meditation does for other people.

The ferry from Nanaimo to Vancouver suffered none of the directional indecision of the first one. It was a huge and impressive and well-appointed vessel, and before it even left the dock, people were sprawled on deck in the sun, or unwrapping sandwiches in the covered solariums in the bow and stern, or napping inside on one of the padded benches. There was a video game room for the youngsters, and TVs showing *Coronation Street*, a long-running British serial drama, and several snack bars. Out the window the sea slid by, and the snow-capped mountains across the strait grew larger, and finally we sidled into Horseshoe Bay northwest of Vancouver and I was back on the continent.

That night I had dinner with my friend Michael and his wife, Sharon. I first met Michael in 1995 when we had both come to a checkpoint of the Iron Butt Rally to see the riders arrive, check in, plan the next leg, and grab a few winks before setting out again on that 11-day, 11,000-mile exercise in self-abuse. Michael would later ride the Rally himself, proving that even the nicest, most rational-seeming people can fall prey to strange and dark urges.

Michael and Sharon fed me lavishly, Michael and I talked into the night, and after our goodbyes I checked into a business hotel nearby and slept soundly.

On my final day in Canada I went to Trev Deeley's Harley dealership in Vancouver, also home to the Deeley Motorcycle Exhibition. There, contrary to my expectations, I found no Harleys on display, but instead a collection of rare and classic British bikes in an exhibition called End of Empire, about the decline of the British motorcycle industry ("A cautionary tale eerily reflective of today's near collapse of the US automotive industry!"). If you're headed that way soon, don't miss it.

I managed to tear myself away around noon and headed south. The GPS said I had a long drive ahead of me if I wanted to get home that night, but every time I thought about stopping a little voice said, "Go on, just a few more miles, then get a motel." That, of course, turned into an all-nighter, and I got home just before 11 p.m., after an 11-hour drive that probably explains why I haven't been fully awake for the last two days.

I have a vague sense of dread that the credit-card bill for all this will beggar me for the next year. But it was worth it. And in a year I'll be ready to go back. Hell, I'm ready now.

But first, I'm going back to bed.

Never Let The Truth Get In
The Way Of A Good Story

(TREAD LIFE, 2009)

I went to Daytona in 1976 to race in the Novice class on my TZ250. Two other racers and I pooled our resources and rented a garage in the pit area for the week. Things were a lot cheaper back then.

Garaged next to us was the Yamaha team, where Kel Carruthers was looking after Kenny Roberts' bikes. Kenny's dad Buster was there, too. So was Ray Hook, who made Blendzall two-stroke oil. Blendzall was the oil of choice back then. Rumor has it the Yamaha guys dumped out the oil in the Yamalube bottles displayed prominently in their garage and filled them with Blendzall when nobody was looking.

Kenny, Buster, and Ray were all from Modesto, California. The guy I was working for at the time, who I'd come to Daytona with, was also from Modesto, and he and Ray were buddies, as were Ray and Buster, so there was occasional coming and going between the Yamaha garage and ours.

That was the first year the AMA required mufflers on roadracers. The stated reason was something along the lines of "less sound, more ground," although how that applied to a superspeedway like Daytona was a mystery to one and all.

When I arrived at the track for the first day of practice, walking around the pits I saw three or four brands of expansion chambers for sale with built-in mufflers. They'd been tuned to work with them, and subsequent lap times showed they gave up little or nothing to the un-muffled pipes everyone had run last year.

Strapped for cash, I had hacksawed the stingers off my expansion chambers and replaced them with generic weld-on mufflers packed with fiberglass. Even I figured this wasn't going to work very well, and I was right. I spent a couple of days trying to get my bike going as fast as it did the year before, with no success.

One afternoon, while I was moping around the garage between practices, Buster Roberts dropped by. He asked how I was doing, and I told him about my lack of speed, and my muffler problem.

Buster and I surmised a bit, and one or the other of us suggested my cylinders might have been ported too radically (or perhaps the word was "inexpertly") to work with mufflers. That was entirely possible, since I did my own port work back then. But I only had the one set of cylinders anyway, so I was stuck with them.

Then Buster said something that floored me. Would I like to borrow a spare set of Kenny's 250 cylinders?

You know that scene in the western where the bad guy walks into the saloon and the piano stops, and everybody's head swivels toward the door? That was pretty much the effect Buster's words had on everyone standing nearby.

I was so surprised that I said something I meant to come out more or less like *Why, yes, Buster, I would, thank you*, but probably sounded like

I was choking on a chicken bone. Buster went next door and a minute later came back and handed me a box containing a cylinder block for a TZ250.

You have to understand that in those days Kenny Roberts was a god. So was Kel Carruthers, who tuned Kenny's bikes. Between the two of them, they were knocking American roadracing on its ear. Rumors abounded about unobtanium parts, magic ignitions, port timing developed by NASA—everyone was certain Kel knew something nobody else did, and that was one of the reasons why Kenny and his bikes were so damn fast.

So when Buster handed me that cylinder block, it was like an angel handing Indiana Jones the Ark and saying, "Go ahead, take a peek inside."

I opened the box and lifted the block out. The first thing I noticed was the ports. They were rough cast, not like the ones in my cylinders that I'd labored over for hours, smoothing the walls with a Dremel tool and jeweler's files.

I grabbed the dial caliper out of my toolbox and measured the port heights and widths. I knew the stock dimensions by heart, and one by one they came up on the dial.

By now I had an audience. "Well?" someone demanded. "Stock," I said, shaking my head. "They're stock."

I thanked Buster for his generosity but decided to stick with my own cylinders. My race didn't go that well. I qualified at the back of the first wave, and finished downfield from there. My bike ran poorly, and by the time I saw the checkered flag I was more than ready for the race to be over.

Kenny Roberts' day didn't go that well, either. A tire failure in the 200 caused him to crash, and Johnny Cecotto ran away with the race. I snapped a picture of Roberts after the race, a minute after he climbed off the bike and pulled off his helmet, exposing the strips of duct tape he used to keep his hair out of his eyes.

After that race our career paths, Kenny Roberts' and mine, diverged. I raced in the AMA for another year or so, then hung up my leathers and eventually became a writer. Kenny Roberts went to Europe, kicked a lot of European road-racing ass, and eventually became a legend.

Years later, when I worked for *Cycle Guide*, I got a chance to interview him for an hour or so at Willow Springs Raceway. I meant to ask him about that cylinder block Buster handed me back in 1976, but I never got around to it.

To this day I can't say for sure whether Buster had picked up the wrong box, or if he was just offering me a new stock cylinder block to replace the one I'd butchered.

But I suspect the truth is that he picked up the right box, that Kenny Roberts ran out-of-the-box cylinders on his 250. After all, why even bring stock cylinders to a race if the ones on the race bike were ported? Why not just bring another set or two of ported cylinders?

I'll probably never know. And you know what? I don't care. In fact, I think the reason why I didn't ask Kenny when I had the chance is I like my version of the truth. And you have to admit, it makes a helluva good story.

Just Flat Amazing

(TREAD LIFE, 2009)

I just watched the Springfield Mile, which I taped off Speed TV last Sunday. I'd been saving it, like a tasty dessert, and tonight the time seemed right to indulge myself.

I've been a flattrack fan for many years, but since I moved to Oregon I've managed to see only one race, a National TT at Castle Rock, Washington, in the late 1980s. Dave Despain was the announcer for the Springfield broadcast, and they could not have chosen a better person for the job. Despain knows flattrack like Vin Scully knows baseball. Working with him was Steve Morehead, a racer I once saw do the near impossible—or so it would have been for me—at Ascot Speedway in Gardena, California.

It was a night race, and practice commenced in the afternoon. Dirt tracks like Ascot change with the temperature and the humidity, so that the surface you practice and time-trial on might well disappear by the time the heat races and main finally flag off.

Ascot was like that. It's a little known fact that they got the dirt for the track from a nearby cemetery. Coming as it did from as much as six feet under, it had a lot of clay in it, and when it was not too dry, not too moist, but just right, it offered phenomenal traction.

Morehead went out in practice and his bike was all over the place. It wouldn't steer going into the corners, and it wouldn't hook up coming out of them. It was full-on dark, with the lights lining the track blazing, as he went out for his last session. He might have been hoping the track would come to him as night fell and the surface got tackier, but it didn't.

I was in the pits that night. A lot of people think there's nothing particularly complicated about flattrack racing—go straight, turn left, go straight, turn left; repeat until checkered flag—but like a lot of things that look simple at first glance, it's not. Bike set-up is critical, as is knowing the track. As I walked past Morehead's pit he rolled in, put his bike up on the stand, and dove into his toolbox. In the space of five minutes, he slid the fork tubes up in the clamps to quicken up the steering; changed the gearing, which also changed the wheelbase; put on a different set of shocks, which changed the rear ride height and thus the front/rear weight distribution; and changed the air pressure in both of the tires.

The rule of thumb in race tuning is never change more than one thing at a time. That way, if the bike is faster or slower, you know exactly what you did that made it that way. There wasn't time to do it that way, though—there never is at a flattrack race—so Morehead went ahead and did everything at once.

And damned if they weren't all the right things to do. The bike hooked up, it steered, and it was fast. Morehead had a good night, I recall. So did I. I'd seen a master at work. What looked like a desperate hail-Mary move was in fact the practical application of years of experience. I never forgot it.

Years later, I got in touch with Morehead to see if he'd be willing to answer some questions about flattrack racing. I was writing my second mystery novel, *Hotshoe*, which takes place on the flattrack circuit, and I wanted to make sure I got all the racing details right.

He was good enough to spend an hour or so on the phone with me, and at some point in the rambling conversation I mentioned that night at Ascot. He remembered it. He remembered every change he'd made to the bike, too. And to my everlasting astonishment, he even remembered me, standing there watching him, taking in every detail.

So flattrack really is very simple after all. Go straight, turn left. Remember the minutest detail of every race you've ever run, including the track conditions, the chassis set-up and gearing of the bike, and some guy you've never seen before or since standing there gawking as you pretty much change everything on your bike but the gas cap. Go straight, turn left. Repeat until checkered flag.

Moto-Archeology

(TREAD LIFE, 2011)

Today I got ambitious and tackled a long-delayed clean-up in the garage. I had six or seven large boxes full of motorcycle stuff I've been carrying from house to house for years without looking inside to see if what they contained was worth keeping. Here's a partial list of what I found:

• A complete valve-shim set for air-cooled, two-valve, four-cylinder, GS-series Suzuki engines

• A 35mm film can full of valve shims, both opening and closing, from my Ducati 900 SS Darmah

• A header-pipe wrench for the same Ducati

• The speedometer from my 1970 R5 Yamaha

• A set of valve-cover bolt seals from my CBX

• Factory valve-shim tools for the CBX and the CB900F I once owned

• A box of racing spark plugs from my TZ250

• A pair of new rear-shock springs for a CB400F

• A single gasket for the top cover of one of the CB400F's carbs

• A complete set of Mikuni hex main jets from 110 to 380, a pair of each

• The cover for the air-cooled clutch of a 1974 TZ250A

• An exhaust valve from a Honda CR110 50cc production roadracer I once bought in boxes for $400 and later sold in the same boxes for $600, congratulating myself on making a $200 profit on a bike that would become a rare and insanely valuable classic 10 years later

• Several pages of notes from my racing days containing detailed port dimensions of the RD350 I ran in the production race at Daytona in 1975; the same dimensions for a TZ750; gearing, tire pressures, and fast lap times for a 1974 race at Sears Point and another in 1975 at Laguna Seca; and notes from my 1975 Daytona Novice race (best practice lap time, 2m 31s; gearing on the TZ, 15/34; premix ratio, 20:1 Castrol R-30; 290 main jets; tire pressures, 30/32; and the reminder that the 76-mile Novice race burned about four gallons of gas)

When I started the garage clean-up, I told myself if I hadn't used something in the last two years, out it went. Everything listed above fit into that category. But I figure since I actually did toss six boxes of junk, I could keep just one little one, taped shut and marked DO NOT TRASH, EVER!!! in thick felt-tip marker. I defy you to tell me you wouldn't have done the same.

Zen And The Art Of Motorcyclist Maintenance

(TREAD LIFE, 2009)

I wrote a while ago about back problems keeping me off the bike. A talk with my chiropractor convinced me the solution was to sell my V-Strom and get a cruiser. The financial climate being what it is, that's not going to happen. So I started thinking about other ways to deal with the situation.

I did some research on the web and found a number of exercises designed to help torn back muscles heal, and to help weak ones get stronger. The kind of injury I had was common among athletes, not just former motojournalists who had pushed the envelope to the point of tearing once too often.

I actually found this information several months ago, but hadn't followed the exercise plan. Or rather, I had followed it too diligently. I got some weights and started using them every day. That, as it turned out, just created another problem. The pain got worse.

I know now that I overworked the injured muscles, and didn't give them time to recover between workouts. So it was back to the chiropractor for a couple of lengths of something called Theraband, essentially a flat strip of stretchy rubber used for light, low-impact muscle and joint rehabilitation.

I've been using it every other day—no more often than that—for about a month now, and the improvement has been remarkable. Not only are my arms and back stronger, I can ride farther without pain than I could six months ago, and I feel less fatigued at the end of the ride.

The point of all this is that I'm finally learning, at the ripe old age of 57, to take it easy on myself. It's my inclination to charge straight at any problem with all guns blazing; that's what got me through the injuries I sustained after the Willow Springs crash in 1986, and the car crash in 2006. I was a rehab fiend both times, and among the rewards was the astonished look on the faces of several doctors at how fast I bounced back.

But some problems can't be solved by full-frontal assaults. You have to creep up on them, and nail them when they aren't looking. You've heard that saying about how "old age and cunning beats youth and enthusiasm"? It's true.

There's also a bit of Zen going on here. As a freelance writer, I'm always looking ahead—to the next story, the next interview, the next paycheck. The now tends to get lost in the concern over the later. In my imperfect understanding of Zen, however, the now is all there is; the past is gone, and the future isn't here yet, and when it arrives, it's the now.

Lately I've been working on being mindful of what's going on right now. When I ride, I try to think about how the ride is going right now, and not about how much it'll suck if my back starts to hurt; that hasn't happened yet, and it might not happen at all. And if it does there's not much I can do about it anyway—why let it affect what's happening now?

So I'm keeping the V-Strom. I have it set up just the way I want it, it's paid for—a huge plus for any bike—and the Sargent seat, well-shaped but originally pretty firm, has finally broken in completely. Either that, or I have permanent nerve damage in my ass.

I'm even thinking of taking another trip to Canada before the summer is out, this time on the bike instead of in the car. When I first entertained the idea, I immediately thought, *What if my back starts hurting? What if the bike breaks down? What if...?*

Then I stopped, took a deep breath, closed my eyes, and thought, *What if it's the best ride ever?*

Motorcycling Lessons Learned

(TREAD LIFE, 2009)

On one of the forums I visit now and then, someone started a thread by asking for responses to the question, "How old are you and how has your riding changed, or has it?" I jotted down a few things that came to mind right away, then the more I thought about it, the longer the list got. This was my answer:

• I'm 57 (for a couple of months more), and I've been riding for 41 of those years.

• Yes, my riding has changed.

• I no longer ride at night.

• I no longer have to be the first guy there.

• I no longer care about anyone's pace but my own.

• I no longer try to keep up with anyone who passes me.

• I no longer feel the need to prove anything to anybody.

• I'm 100 percent ATGATT. (For the uninitiated, that's an acronym for "all the gear, all the time," "gear" being riding gear—helmet, armored jacket and pants, gloves, boots.)

• I'm convinced that most motorcycles need much bigger and brighter taillights.

• I'm intrigued by big scooters and sidecars and I don't care who knows it.

• It's more fun to ride a small bike as fast as it'll go than it is to ride a big one way too fast.

• It's more fun to stop for coffee or to stretch and sightsee every 50 or 100 miles and arrive in time for a late dinner than it is to ride 400 miles in one shot and get there by lunchtime.

A Flea On The Tiger's Back

(TREAD LIFE, 2010)

If someone were to offer me a track day on Valentino Rossi's Yamaha M1 MotoGP bike today, I wouldn't have to think about my answer. I'm too old to go haring around a racetrack on an expert-level racebike, I'm not even flexible enough to fit on it, and I couldn't go anywhere near fast enough to appreciate it for what it is. So I'd say thanks, but no, thanks.

In 1986 someone asked me a similar question and I didn't have to think about my answer then, either. I said, "Hell yes!"

The bike in question was also a Yamaha, a distant ancestor of the M1—the TZ750. During its heyday, the 750cc four-cylinder two-stroke had a reputation for being vicious, nasty, hard to ride, and nearly unmanageable in all but the most expert hands. According to someone who ought to know, it was overweight, it didn't steer, and no matter how well set up the suspension was, it wobbled like a shopping cart with a bent wheel.

That someone was Kenny Roberts. And when KR talks, you listen. Especially when he says of the TZ750, "This bike spit me down the road more times than any other bike I've ever raced."

Roberts and a 1977-vintage TZ750 owned by Yamaha racing director Ken Clark, along with two-time AMA Superbike champ Wes Cooley and his 1980 title-winning Yoshimura GS1000 Suzuki Superbike owned by Craig Vetter, had been invited to Willow Springs Raceway in Rosamond, California, to take part in one of *Cycle Guide*'s high-concept feature stories, this one comparing the TZ and the GS with their approximate street-going counterparts, the FZ750 and GSX-R750. The general idea was to inflate the egos of sportbike riders by showing them how like actual race motorcycles their streetbikes were.

A flimsy premise, yes, but it got us two days at Willow, and the opportunity to ride two legendary racebikes.

I wrote the story in *CG*, and was so busy taking notes that I remember only a little bit of what went on during those two days. I remember catching editor Jim Miller going into a slow left-hander, diving inside him, and whacking the throttle on the Yosh Suzuki as I passed him. Later he said the sound that erupted from the open megaphone nearly blasted him out of the saddle of the GSX-R750.

I remember sitting on the dusty floor of a bare room under the timing tower—there was no furniture, not even chairs—interviewing Roberts about the TZ750, his racing career, and anything else that came to mind. I probably asked him what his favorite color was—when you get a guy like KR to sit down for a Q&A, you milk it for all you can.

But the thing I remember most is walking up to that TZ750, pulling in the clutch, thumbing the choke lever, toeing the gear lever down into second, pushing the bike down the pit lane, dropping the clutch, and hearing the dry clutch rattle and the engine burble for a few seconds before it lit up with a deafening staccato shriek that shot an entire day's supply of adrenalin through me in a second.

I'd raced a 1974 TZ250 about a decade earlier, and the TZ750 was not so far removed from it that everything was unfamiliar—the hard rubber grips, the reversed shift pattern, the bark of the muffled expansion chambers all triggered long-buried sense memories. But after I'd put a cautious warm-up lap under my belt and twisted the grip all the way for the first time as I hit the main straight, it was like nothing I'd ever experienced before or since.

The bike was geared for Daytona or some other high-speed track; at Willow it was topped out in fourth by the time turn one came up, with fifth and sixth unusable. It still tripped the radar gun at nearly 150.

When I hit the brakes the bike stopped *right now*, about 50 yards sooner than I'd expected. As I built up speed I braked later and later, and every time, the TZ stopped so hard my eyeballs flattened against the inside of my faceshield. In the corners it felt like it was on rails, and changed direction so quickly and easily I couldn't reconcile it with what Roberts had been saying about it only an hour before.

The power was astonishing; the engine came on the ports with the suddenness of a punch in the face. No hesitation, no lean spot as it made the transition; below the powerband there was decent power, then in the blink of an eye there was *holyshiiiit*-loads of power. Exhilarating is too weak a word to describe the sensation of riding it. It was, as the kids say today, awesome.

Back in the pits I babbled on about how fast it was and how easy it was to ride—until Dain Gingerelli pointed out that I hadn't been riding it at anywhere near a race pace. He was right, of course. I'd been going as fast as I'd dared on someone else's rare and expensive race bike, but the more I thought about it, the happier I was that I hadn't simply embarrassed myself by fouling a plug—or my leathers.

Later that day I got to watch Roberts on the TZ. He hadn't rid-

den one in years—he'd only ever ridden this one once, five years earlier—but despite that, and the fact that there was nothing at stake but a
magazine story he'd probably never read anyway, he flew around Willow like a man possessed.

I got to ride one legend that day, and see another put on a show.
Not bad, even if I never got going fast enough to get the TZ's attention.

Good Night, Sweet Prints

(TREAD LIFE, 2009)

I picked up my first motorcycle magazine sometime in the 1960s, when I was still in high school. It was probably a *Cycle World*, but it could have been a *Cycle*, too. It doesn't matter. I was hooked. From that moment on I bought, read, and saved almost every bike mag I got my hands on.

Eventually the accumulation of magazines got out of hand. Last year, when I moved from a house I'd lived in for 15 years to this one, I went down to the basement where they were piled with the intent of boxing all of them to take with me.

It took about 10 minutes to realize that the sheer effort of lugging all those magazines up the stairs would take years off my life if it didn't kill me outright. So I started two piles, the keepers and the recyclers. I still had to haul all of them upstairs, but only a fraction of them had to be carried to the new house.

These days I'm wondering if I did the right thing by tossing so many of them. That's because motorcycle magazines, along with the rest of the print media, are on the ropes, thanks mostly to what you're doing right now—reading this on the internet.

The internet has a number of built-in advantages over print. The internet is not a physical product. It's not printed on paper, and it doesn't have to be mailed to the reader, or delivered by truck to a newsstand. So it's cheaper to produce and distribute right from the start.

In addition, the internet is immediate. Most motorcycle magazines come out six, nine, or 12 times a year. Some websites are updated that many times each day, making the idea of "news" in the context of a monthly magazine laughable.

The inevitable result of this is that magazines have had to become more like websites, with more flashy graphics to grab your attention and fewer words to make you stop and think.

Cook Neilson, the former editor of *Cycle*, said it best in an interview on motohistory.net, when asked for his thoughts on motorcycle journalism today, and whether he'd be comfortable getting back into it full-time:

> Everything's different not just in the publishing world; it's different in the WHOLE world. The competition out there for eyeballs is ferocious: TV, video games, the Internet, all different kinds of other magazines. So at the same time the motorcycle magazine press is becoming more and more stratified and "niche-ified," it is being forced to move faster and faster. It strikes me that it's not as contemplative as it used to be, and I feel the decibel level has gone up. There are pluses, though. The quality of the graphics is much stronger than it used to be. Cycle World and Roadracer X both look terrific, and they both seem to have unlimited color budgets, which we never had. My sense is that circumstances are forcing the publishers and editors to go for maximum impact,

all the time. I read a while ago that Roadracer X didn't feature the Suzuki race bikes on their covers as much as they otherwise would have because the Suzukis are blue and therefore don't have the kind of eye-catching instant newsstand appeal that red or yellow bikes produce. I understand that speed, immediacy, loudness, urgency, and impact are seen as essential. I'm not sure I like it. Phil [Schilling, who succeeded Neilson as Cycle's editor] and I have talked about this quite a bit; I'm not sure he likes it either. But it is what it is.

What Neilson didn't say is what many magazine publishers are finding out every day, which is that in addition to print magazines taking on more and more of the characteristics of the internet—"speed, immediacy, loudness, urgency, and impact"—at the same time the internet is taking advertising revenue away from the print media in buckets.

For example, newspapers make a lot of money from classified ads—or they did, until Craigslist came along and offered to post those same ads on the internet, where they're accessible to far more readers in many more places than any newspaper can hope to reach, for free.

Advertising pays a magazine's bills, and advertising space in a magazine is sold based on the number of people who read the magazine. The more readers the magazine has, the more it can charge for ads. Since the point of advertising is to reach as many people as possible, as readers migrate to the web so will advertisers, leaving behind them a huge hole in the print magazines' ad revenues.

I'm not suggesting motorcycle magazines are breathing their last, although several that I'm familiar with are looking a bit pale and listless lately. As someone who makes his living writing for them, I certainly wish them a long and happy life.

I also wish I had back all those magazines I threw out.

Crazy George

(JALOPNIK, 2018)

He came in about once a week, opening the front door and then pausing there for a few seconds with an expression anyone past a certain age can relate to: *Now, what did I come in here for?* He wore thick glasses that looked like he cleaned them with steel wool; one lens was cracked. He wore greasy, baggy jeans with rolled-up cuffs, and sometimes he was shirtless. His beard sprouted from his face like weeds in an untended garden. It was easy to see why everyone called him Crazy George.

After he came to, he'd shuffle along the rows of new Hondas and Kawasakis parked in the showroom of Marin Motorsports, where I was working. I was behind the parts counter most of the time, but also played salesman when the real one was busy. If there was nobody else around I'd ask George if he needed anything, and if he answered at all, he'd say he was just looking. Then out of nowhere he's ask me a question about a new bike—"Did they change the cam timing on this year's model?" or "What's the speed rating of the tires on that one?"—that had me scratching my head, not just because I didn't know the answer, but because he looked like he'd be out of his depth timing the operation of a washcloth and a bar of soap.

George Disteel—that was his real name—wasn't always an eccentric who occasionally wandered into motorcycle shops like a stray cat begging for a bowl of milk. Some of the details of his early life—and in fact his entire life—qualify as either rumor or conjecture, but it's known with reasonable certainty that he was born in Pennsylvania in 1904 and served in the military before settling in Marin County, California, in the 1940s. Then as now, Marin was a great place to own a motorcycle. A short ride west got you to Highway 1 on the spectacular coast, or south to San Francisco, or north to wine country. The jewel in the Marin crown was Mount Tamalpais, whose 2500-foot elevation offered a sweeping view of the Bay Area, with the bonus of a twisty, challenging road to the summit and back.

Disteel worked as a carpenter when has wasn't traipsing all over Marin on foot, or on a bicycle or a motorcycle. A fitness freak before it was fashionable, he exercised vigorously every day and ate only natural foods. He lived in a tumbledown shack surrounded by running and non-running motorcycles, including the Vincent he rode whenever the mood struck him.

Then, abruptly, Disteel moved out of the shack and warehoused the bikes. He later confided to a coworker that his son had been killed in a motorcycle accident, though it's not known if he ever actually had a son. The event, real or imagined, triggered a dormant hoarding gene, and Disteel began collecting rifles, medical instruments, radios, photographic equipment, newspapers—and motorcycles.

The story goes that after the death of his son, Disteel became obsessed with buying up motorcycles and squirreling them away to prevent other young men from suffering the same fate. He bought a variety of bikes, but preferred Vincents. Despite his disheveled appearance and squalid living conditions, he had made a bundle investing in real estate, and used the proceeds to fund his mania.

After he retired from the carpentry trade he bounced around, first as a watchman for an automobile junk yard and later as a caretaker at the Boyd Museum in San Rafael, a gig that included free lodging. His hoarding cost him both positions, and reduced him to sleeping in his car, a 1952 Hudson packed to the window sills with all his belongings and parked out back of the Boyd. After the cops kicked him out of there, he trashed the car and moved to a flophouse across the Golden Gate in San Francisco.

But the lure of Marin County was strong, and Disteel would find his way back there occasionally, on foot if necessary. This is where I became aware of him, if not friends with him. Marin Motorsports was one of his regular stops, where he'd come to look at the new bikes, ask his arcane questions, and then leave as silently as he'd arrived. Marin being what it was, he was not only tolerated, but held in the sort of fond esteem reserved for three-legged dogs and really ugly buildings.

One day in 1978 he came in, did his rounds of the new bikes, and then stepped up to the parts counter where I was killing time. "How much for that Gold Wing?" he said, pointing to a GL1000. I looked around the showroom for Dennis, the salesman, but he wasn't there, so I went to the sales desk and got out the price sheet. I read him the suggested retail, a price nobody with two brain cells to rub together would pay. He said, "Okay," and left.

The next day he came back and handed me a check for some odd amount, like $623.46. "A deposit," he said. "I'll come back with the rest next week." Then he was gone. When I told the owner of shop about it later he laughed, told me a few Crazy George stories, and said the check was probably bogus. But the bank said it was good, so I started a folder for the sale and rolled the bike out back to the service department to be prepped for delivery.

Disteel never came back. A few weeks later he walked out the front door of his flop in San Francisco and dropped dead on the sidewalk, aged 74. The cause of death was determined to be heart failure and emphysema. He had no ID on him, and was initially listed as a John Doe.

It was soon determined that Disteel wasn't just another vagrant down on his luck. When he was identified, and his papers were located and examined, it turned out he owned a lot of real estate—more than two dozen properties—and had a warehouse in Cotati, north of San Rafael, full of motorcycles.

For years rumors had swirled around Crazy George's obsession with Vincents and other superbikes, and the discovery of a cache of them set off a frenzy, especially in the cult-like local Vincent community.

But when the bikes were located and moved to an auction house to be sold off, potential buyers were shocked to see the condition many of them were in—rusty, dirty, with rotten tires, and spotted with chicken shit, hardly worth the few salvageable parts on them. Still, most were bought at the auction and some of the less damaged ones were later restored, but there never was anything like the treasure trove of pristine classic bikes rumor insisted Disteel had stashed away.

Eventually more warehouses full of Disteel's junk were found, but most of their contents were of interest only to the owners of quaint antique stores in seaside tourist towns, or other hoarders. To this day, however, there are those who insist there are more stashes of vintage bikes that have yet to be uncovered.

I've tried to recall what happened to that Gold Wing Disteel gave me a deposit on, but I can't. I'd like to think it went back on the showroom floor and was bought by someone who rode the hell out of it.

Whatever happened to it, at least it didn't end up sitting in one of Crazy George's warehouses, slowly turning to rust.

Scents of Wonder

(TREAD LIFE, 2009)

Smell is a potent wizard that transports us across thousands of miles and all the years we have lived.
—Helen Keller

One of the more frequently cited reasons for riding a motorcycle instead of driving a car is that the car isolates you from your environment, while the motorcycle makes you part of it. If you've ever ridden through farm country and inhaled the rich, earthy aroma of a freshly plowed field, or sniffed the moisture-laden air that precedes the rain long before the first drops hit your faceshield, you know this to be true.

This evening I sat out on the deck tossing the ball for Daisy, Tread Life's editorial assistant and morale officer. It had rained in the morning and showered on and off into the early afternoon. Thick clouds bowled along overhead on a breeze that brought with it the first hint of the change of seasons.

Something about those clouds, and the wind, and the slant of the sun, made me a little sad. The summers here are too brief, and this one is almost over. The rain is coming back soon, and with it days of gray skies, morning chill, and early nightfall. Time to dig out the electric vest and the heavy gloves, and put a fresh layer of Sno Seal on my boots.

But the breeze brought something else—a memory, one of Helen Keller's "potent wizards." A memory, almost a palpable sensation, of the desert in late autumn, with scattered patches of green dotting the sandy monotony, a warm wind blowing, that feeling of the riding season slipping away, and a motorcycle ride I took almost eight years ago.

For a number of years, around this time, the word would go out on the long-distance riders mailing list announcing the Chiliburger Run, held around the first of October at the Riverside Inn in Horseshoe Bend, Idaho. What began as a couple of people meeting there for lunch eventually morphed into a full-scale invasion of the restaurant by LD riders who live by the motto, "Live to ride, ride to eat."

In 2001, I bought a Honda ST1100 from Dale "Warchild" Wilson, a former Iron Butt Rally rider and currently the Iron Butt Association's technical inspector, etiquette adviser, and fool frightener. It was tricked out for rally riding, with fearsomely bright driving lights and an auxiliary gas tank that brought the total fuel capacity to 11 gallons, giving it a range between fill-ups of more than 400 miles.

The Chiliburger Run was accurately—and bluntly—billed as "the last chance for a ride before the weather in the Northwest turns to shit." By that time of year the eastern Oregon desert, which lies between me and Horseshoe Bend, could in the course of a single day serve up the entire weather menu, from scaring heat to blizzards. One year I rode through a rainstorm like a car wash, and an hour later sat gasping in the shimmering heat under the stingy shade of a lean-to in a rest stop where the only amenities were a trash can, and a sign prohibiting dumping trash in it.

The ST was the perfect sport-touring mount, an immensely capable bike whose limits I never discovered, mainly because I couldn't exploit the 400-mile range with my 150-mile ass. Still, while as a rule I have no use for the desert, I approached the edge of it with a sense of anticipation. I was on a great bike, and I had all day to get to my hotel in Boise, and nothing to do the next day but get myself to the Riverside Inn and go *mano a mano* with a chiliburger the size of a catcher's mitt.

As I recall, the weather that year was particularly fine. It wasn't too hot, and the few hardy things that bloom in the desert, however fleetingly, were getting on with doing just that.

Huge, brilliant white clouds floated overhead, spanning the horizons, blotting out the sun one minute and scudding out of the way the next. The air sometimes smelled like that peculiar odor of dust and moisture that means rain, but no rain fell. The season was turning in the desert, and I was alone on a motorcycle in the middle of nowhere, miles from help if I needed it, with nothing between me and disaster but a couple of improbably small patches of rubber and the laws of physics.

If you ever find yourself in that position, and you don't feel more alive than you've ever felt, then you're already dead.

I got to Boise that evening, defeated the chiliburger fair and square the next day, and the day after that headed home. Between Burns and Bend I hooked up with a trio of 18-wheelers barreling along nose-to-tail at 80 mph. I tucked in behind the last one in line, close enough to get a tow from the draft but far enough behind and to the side that I could see up ahead and drop back to safety in time if I needed to. I arrived home late that night by the blazing light of a pair of PIAA tree-burners.

Where I live now is about as much like the desert as a horse is like a turtle, so I can't really explain how the smell of a breeze from the Pacific Ocean this evening reminded of a ride across eastern Oregon. All I can say for sure is it conjured up the past, and gave me a part of my life to live all over again, a part I'd all but forgotten.

Maybe that's why Helen Keller called smells "wizards," because if that isn't magic, I don't know what is.

The Dog And The Hog

(TREAD LIFE, 2009)

We all have little secrets we'd prefer no one else knew. Maybe your iPod is full of Clay Aiken songs, or your nickname in high school was Crater Face.

Me? I like sidehacks.

I really should know better, too. When I worked at *Rider* I had a chance to put some miles on two sidehacks, one a factory-built Harley Electra Glide rig and the other a BMW K100-based EML. I learned that sidehacks combine the very worst traits of cars and motorcycles into a single machine that lacks any of their virtues.

The EML outfit was made in Germany, and as you'd expect, it was a lot more technically sophisticated than the Harley. It had fuel injection, shaft drive, a leading-link front end, and a sidecar that looked like it had been stolen from the German Olympic bobsled team. It rolled on what appeared to be a car tire in the back, and had a similar square-edged tire up front.

It's my guess that the front tire accounted for why the EML was so little fun to ride. Sidehacks are known for heavy steering, but this one was awful. Even with the leading-link front end, the front tire leaned slightly from side to side when I turned the handlebar. Each time I did, it felt as if the bike was resisting being tilted up on that square edge. A rounder profile might have solved the problem, but the rig had to go back before I had a chance to find out.

Compared to the EML, the Harley was as sophisticated as a claw hammer. They even left the sidestand on the Glide when they bolted the sidecar up to it. The fork was the same telescopic unit found on all the other baggers, and the sidecar had that nose-wrinkling fiberglass smell, as well as a number of sharp rivet heads poking into the interior, like an iron maiden with a windscreen. It was a thing of beauty, though, with a timeless style that made me grin every time I thought about anyone still making something that weird and wonderful.

The Harley was even harder to ride than the EML. Every time I turned the handlebar the entire rig felt like it was winding itself up like a big spring. The sidecar lagged on acceleration, pulling the rig to the right, and although the sidecar wheel had a brake, the sidecar tried to pass me whenever I braked, pulling to the left. At first it was all I could do to ride it a block without veering into oncoming traffic or colliding with parked cars.

But the Harley had something the EML didn't, and probably never would have. It had the same effect on people as a string of circus elephants marching down Main Street. Adults stopped and stared, little kids pointed and laughed. I felt like I ought to be wearing jodhpurs and a pith helmet, with a comical sidekick named Bud or Stumpy in the sidecar. Every ride was an adventure, and after a while I forgot what a peg-legged goat the thing was, and grew to like it.

I rode it from Southern California to Las Vegas to attend the auction of the Steve McQueen estate at some garish casino on the strip. I'm usually a frugal packer when it comes to bike travel, but with the Harley I filled the sidecar with all the luggage I owned and still had enough room left over for a beach ball and a grandfather clock.

When I got to the outskirts of Vegas and hit the first stoplight, I put my foot down. Then I started laughing. The man in the car next to me glanced over at me as if he thought I was losing my mind.

What I remember best about the Harley, though, is how my old dog Steve took to it. Steve didn't care for motorcycles one bit. He stayed in the garage during the day when I was at work—the landlord's rules, not mine—and every time I brought a bike home he'd hide in the corner behind the workbench until I shut off the engine, then come creeping out to greet me.

He did the same thing when I brought the Harley home for the first time, and every time after that—until one day I picked him up, all 60 quivering pounds of him, and put him in the sidecar.

I could almost see the cartoon light bulb go on over his head. *Huh. This isn't so bad.*

I clipped a short leash to his collar and tied it off to the grab rail in the sidecar. He just about tore it loose when I stared the engine, but by the end of the driveway he had settled back into the padded seat. *Okay, maybe once around the block.*

That's all it took. He was hooked.

For the rest of the time I had the Harley, as soon as I opened the garage door a big red dog would come charging out and leap into the sidecar. Then one day I came home with just another motorcycle, and he ran and hid behind the workbench until I shut it off.

Steve was a great dog, and lived to be 15 years old. He came with me when I moved to Oregon, where he traded a fenced back yard for five acres of wooded land where he could run and dig and chase deer and quail and do all the things dogs were born to do. I believe he was a happy dog right up until the end.

But I don't think he ever forgave me for giving back the Harley.

How The Honda VFR800 Kept Me On Motorcycles

(JALOPNIK, 2017)

This was the script for every ride I went on for about two years: It starts as a pinpoint of pain, about halfway up my spine and maybe an inch to the right of center. *Nothing to worry about, a little stiffness is all. Keep going.*

Then it blossoms from a pinpoint to a circle, growing bigger and bigger, until it radiates to my shoulder and halfway down my arm. The pain is intense, like a passenger slowly screwing an ice pick into my back, and impossible to ignore. It's hard to hold the throttle steady. *Shit, just 10 minutes this time and I'm all used up.* Turn around, go home, gobble a fistful of Tylenol, and lie down on an ice pack for an hour. *Another wasted ride. Fuck.*

There's a bit of T-shirt wisdom that goes like this: You don't stop riding because you get old, you get old because you stop riding. But what the T-shirt doesn't tell you is this: You eventually get old either way. And if the years don't get you, sometimes bad luck does.

Hang out with any group of old men and odds are the talk will eventually turn to their medical issues. If those old guys are riders, they'll just as likely discuss custom seats, bar risers, taller windscreens, lower pegs—all the ways to make a motorcycle more accommodating to bodies with a lot of miles on their biological odometers.

I spent the last 10 years or so modifying bikes to lessen the effects of some bad stuff that happened way back when. I usually succeeded, but only for a year or two before there were no mods left to do, and the problem came roaring back like a food-truck burrito in the night, and I sold the bike and got another. I even got so fed up I quit riding for a year; I only just got back on a bike, and I felt 10 years younger right away. And the bike I got back on? Surprised the hell out of me.

Soon after a racetrack crash in 1986 sportbikes became a problem for me. A weakened back and shoulder made the lean-forward riding position agonizing. Although I worked at a magazine with garage full of cutting-edge sportbikes—we called it the candy store, and I had the key—I usually rode something more upright home for the night, like a touring bike, a dual-sport, or whatever Harley we had. I more or less successfully talked my way out of going along on any tests that involved sportbikes, especially on racetracks (Willow Springs was my particular *bête noire*), where I was happy to watch from the pit wall and clean the other guys' face shields between sessions.

After going freelance, the bikes I owned all mirrored my preference for the sit-up-and-beg seating position. The aftermarket is thick with options to accomplish this, but some work better than others. Handlebar relocation is easy on bikes with tubular bars. Just find a bend you like, then make sure the control cables and hoses reach and don't stretch or kink at full steering lock. The last bar I put on my Bonneville came off a Yamaha Grizzly quad, and required an extended cable and brake hose kit. It took about two hours of fiddling to do the job.

On bikes with separate clip-on bars above the top clamp, you can get risers that raise the bars an inch, give or take. But most don't change the angle or setback, just the height. Replacement bars are pricey, and some require extended cables and hoses. I have a set of Heli bars on my own bike now in place of the GenMar risers it came with, and they look as good as, and maybe better than, stock, with both rise and setback changes that make them worth the price and the hassle of installation.

Footpegs are more complicated. Lowering them, with either an aftermarket peg kit or by bolting on pegs from some other model, opens up the seating position and is kinder to old, creaky knees like mine. But the shift and brake pedals sometimes don't have enough adjustability to adapt to the new peg position; they're left at an awkward angle that requires you to lift your foot off the peg to brake, or reach awkwardly for the shifter.

Seats make a big comfort difference, especially compared to the crappy seats on many stock bikes; they were designed for showroom appeal, not long-haul riding, but sometimes you don't discover this until the first time you're hours from home with a numb ass. Off-the-shelf aftermarket seats are miles better than many stockers, but for my money custom is the way to go.

Sometimes the most constructive thing you can do is change your own expectations of what you want from a bike, and the kind of riding you want to do with it. I have a lot of friends in the Iron Butt Association, and I went so far as to ride 1023 miles in less than 24 hours to earn my entrance into the asylum.

For a long time, being able to do a Saddlesore 1000 on it was my baseline for any bike I owned. But after my much-altered Bonnie started hurting me, I decided I was through with long-distance riding; I'd make do with banzai backroad runs to the coffee shop on sunny afternoons—

making me a genuine café racer—and the occasional day ride with buddies down the coast and back. I figured as long as I wasn't going to be on the bike all day, ultimate comfort didn't matter that much, so I might as well get something fun.

Right around this time my friend Stephen called. He had a very nice 2000 Honda VFR800—definitely a sportbike, you'll note, and at the time not at the top of my want list—sitting in his garage that he wanted gone. Years ago I'd told him, partly in jest, that if he ever wanted to sell it he should call me first.

Well, he did, and I thought what the hell, let's take it for a spin. It had some sensible mods—bar risers, lower Buell footpegs, a Sargent seat, heated grips, a voltmeter—but was otherwise stock, and eat-off-it clean. And the price? Just $2500. I took it for a ride, felt no pain at all, and a week later it was in my garage.

Ever since slotting Screaming Yellow into my stable I've been enjoying riding again. I can cram as much fun into 30 minutes on a backroad as I ever did on a weekend on the highway. Even if I'm not going as fast as some pimply testosterone junkie on a CBR600RR, I feel like I am, and that's what counts.

Whatever physical issues I used to have with sportbikes have either shifted elsewhere or diminished to such a degree that I feel no back pain at all. Period. I have no explanation for this, nor do I require one. I'm just happy to be back on two wheels.

On The Job

(TREAD LIFE, 2009)

Most people have no idea what it's like to be a writer. I know this because every time someone asks me what I do for a living, and I say I'm a writer, they say, "Oh, you're a writer? That must be so interesting!" Or "fun." Or "exciting."

Being a writer and working from home is, in fact, almost always none of those things. It's mostly work, like any other job, except you don't have to pick up heavy things, deal with the public, or wear a tie—or pants.

And if you think working at home is cool, just remember that also means you live at work.

I originally got into the writing business because I wanted to get into motorcycle races without paying for a ticket. I wrote a letter to *Cycle Guide*, offering to take photos at the San Jose Mile and Laguna Seca if the magazine would get me a press pass. To my astonishment, the sport editor took me up on that offer. Eventually he asked me to write stories to go with my photos, and I more or less backed into my current career.

For the past 21 years I've been a full-time freelancer, which means I hire myself out to various publications on a per-story basis. I come up with an idea and pitch it to an editor, or an editor comes up with an idea and asks me if I'd like to write a story about it. Either way, my livelihood depends on a constant supply of fresh ideas, mine or someone else's.

Sometimes the ideas don't come. That means checks don't come, either. That's when I do one of two things. Plan A is stare a hole in the wall until an idea crawls out of it. Some people can make things happen this way, by sheer force of will. I'm not one of them. Plan B is to go do something else and let the ideas come in their own time, a method that paradoxically combines work with the avoidance of work. In other words, I can ride to a coffee shop, spend the afternoon there reading the paper, and still be technically on the job. I love Plan B.

Some of the work I do is behind the scenes. I edit and copyedit for one of the magazines I write for, and now and then for a book publisher. Writing a magazine or a book is, or should be, a collaborative process. The more eyes that see a story or manuscript before it goes to press, the better the chances are of ferreting out errors of fact, style, grammar, and usage. (The more attentive among you will no doubt find some of these scattered around this very blog. To which I can only reply, where were you when I needed you?)

My own eyes have seen some pretty terrible things in the course of editing, like a recommendation of the Honda Gold Wing as the perfect bike on which to circumvent the globe; the fact that an injured racer took a year off to coalesce at home; the assertion that earthquakes are caused by teutonic plate movement; an exhaustive review of a book about Buells that the reviewer read all the way through without noticing that Buell's first name is spelled Erik, not Eric; and the words *publically*, *desparate*, and *preformance* (which of course should be *publicly*, *desperate*, and *performance*), a clear indication that some writers who pride themselves on an intimate knowledge of the intricacies of automotive and motorcycle technology have not yet figured out how to work their computer's spell checker, or how to navigate a dictionary. (Helpful hint: The words are in alphabetical order.)

Sometimes I don't know whether to laugh or cry.

Either way, it's my job to fix it. This process has been referred to as "making someone else's resumé look good," because when writers whose work you've tuned up want to impress another editor, they won't offer the story as it was submitted—known as raw copy—as proof of their skills, but rather the version someone like me labored over for a couple of hours to turn into something approximating English.

Hey, it's a living.

Actually, it's less of a living now than it used to be, thanks to the internet, which has been siphoning advertising away from print magazines for years, and the current economy, which has only made the internet effect worse by making advertisers afraid to come out from under the bed until the scary monsters go away. Fewer ads mean fewer pages per issue of your favorite magazine, and that means fewer stories an editor needs each month, and that means some really good ideas—some of them mine—die quiet deaths before their time.

I realize that by this point I've painted a grim picture of writing for a living, and you might well be asking yourself why I don't get out of the business. It's a question I've asked myself often as I sat at my desk, losing a staring contest with a blank screen on my laptop, and there's only one answer that makes any sense.

You've heard of people who say they love their job so much they'd do it for free? I'm one of them, and you're reading the proof. There's something about starting with a bunch of unconnected thoughts, and then lining them up in the right order so they make sense, that appeals to me in a way that goes beyond mere enjoyment. When everything is going right, my conscious brain almost steps out of the way, as if something is writing through me, using me as a conduit. You'd think that as a writer I'd be able to convey that feeling more clearly, but I can't. It's impossible to describe, except to say it makes me feel very alive.

Still, I have to consider the practical side of all this. It takes money to keep the lights on around here, and to keep Daisy supplied with tennis balls. There might come a time when I give up writing as a full-time occupation and get a job someplace where I have to wear pants to work.

But I get the feeling that if I ever do, I'll miss the interesting, fun, and exciting life of a freelance writer.

Washington State Tour

If it's Wednesday
this must be Walla Walla

(RIDER)

The state of Washington's tourism board had this idea. Invite a group of motojournalists to ride around and report back to their readers about what a beautiful place Washington is to ride. They invited me, representing *Rider*; Buzz Buzzelli, editor of *American Rider*; and four others, one of whom never showed up. That guy should be kicking himself around the block right about now.

We gathered east of Seattle to pick up rented bikes. I scored a Gold Wing, as black as sin and just as much fun. Buzz got a Road King, Andy from *Motorcycle Escape* a BMW, Nick from the Dutch magazine *Promotor* an FJR1300, and Jim, a freelancer of no fixed affiliation, drew the low card, a Magna with its best days barely visible in the mirrors. Tom, our guide, rode his own FZ6. We saddled up at oh-dark-thirty and headed east.

We rode in a pack past fields and houses shrouded in a wet, late-September fog. Those who hadn't started out in wet-weather gear wished they had. We followed Highway 2 toward Stevens Pass, past towns with names like Sultan, Startup, and Index. The fog cleared as we rode higher, and the sun shone down on rugged mountains clad in fiery fall colors. Construction zones were marked with signs that said "Motorcyclists Use Extreme Caution." Well, of course we do.

Group-think bit the dust early on. At Coles Corner, Buzz, who prefers to ride alone and shuns the beaten path for the road less traveled, went straight when the rest of us went left. Stops for photography soon splintered the rest of group. As the day warmed up I stopped at a small store in Plain to take the liner out of my jacket. A friendly dog visited with two locals relaxing in plastic chairs out front. "Nice dog," said one. "Her mother was a beauty," said the other. "Bob felt real bad when he dropped that tree on 'er." "Last year on my birthday I hit a dog with my truck." Plain's a tough town for dogs.

I missed the lunch rendezvous in Leavenworth. This was concurrent with discovering I'd lost the route map Tom had given out at breakfast. I rode on a bit farther to Wenatchee where I got a sandwich at a supermarket deli and ate it in the shade of a canopy covering stacks of cases of soda pop. From there I steered the Wing north along the west bank of the Columbia. On my side of the river sheer, rocky cliffs came almost to the shoulder of the road and shot straight up. Across the river the bank was wider, with crops planted right up to the base of the cliffs on that side. Where it wasn't irrigated the land had the look of high desert. Take away the water and that's what it would have been—and had been, not that long ago.

Our first night's lodging was in Chelan, at the south end of the long, narrow lake by the same name. Even this late in the year the resort town was hopping. I sat on the balcony of my room making notes and enjoying the cool breeze off the lake as a speedboat scraped a white wake across the glassy water in the distance.

Day two was a long one, with Walla Walla, just six miles from the Oregon border, at the other end. The group did the tourist bit at an overlook above Grand Coulee Dam and then, exhausted by the effort, Buzz, Andy, Nick, and I stopped a few miles later in Electric City for a coffee break. At Pepper Jack's we debated weighty issues like "Working hard, or hardly working?" in the way that only a group of writers on an expense account can, which is to say over several cups of coffee and slices of pie. It wasn't entirely our fault. The waitress was so much fun we hated to leave.

Our first sight of Banks Lake banished any regrets. Start with the towering mesas of Utah's Monument Valley, then fetch a river from Alaska with its deep blue-green water, and lay it at their feet. Nick, from low, flat Holland, was stunned by the stark beauty. "I could spend two weeks here just taking pictures," he said. For the next 50 miles we spent as much time gripping cameras as we did turning throttles. At that rate we really would have been there for two weeks.

We found Tom and Jim waiting for us at the appointed lunch spot in Moses Lake. From our lakeside table we watched jet airliners and huge military transport planes landing and taking off from an airfield in the distance. As experienced motojournalists, all of us were used to clomping into fancy restaurants in our riding gear and covering empty tables with sweaty, bug-stained helmets. The same could not be said for the locals, who eyed us warily. It was here I decided to go on an all-salmon diet for the rest of the trip. These people might be a long way from the ocean, but they knew how to cook fish.

After lunch—and there's no way to sugar-coat this so we don't sound like such a bunch of dopes—we got lost. It was around this time I reminded Buzz to never again kid me about riding with a GPS. A paper map will tell you where you want to go, but it won't tell you where you are, which is exactly what we needed to know. All the roads looked the same, as did the fields and low hills. The only things that changed were the signs pointing to tiny towns that weren't on the maps we had. The towns had funny-sounding names that sounded vaguely Native American. For all we knew they translated to "Aren't we going in circles?" and "We're all going to die here."

Then, on a no-name road in the middle of nowhere, by what I can only assume was the dumbest luck possible, we spotted Tom riding toward us. "Follow me," he said, and we did, like chicks trailing behind a mother hen, all the way to Walla Walla.

The next morning Nick and I had tire issues to deal with. The Weather Channel had been tracking a front moving our way from the northwest that had the potential to make the last two days of our ride soggy ones. I wasn't confident there was enough tread left on the Gold Wing's front tire to cope with rain, and Nick felt the same about the rear tire on his FJR. After breakfast I made some calls and found tires for both of us at USA Honda, a 15-minute ride from our hotel. Brian told us to bring our bikes over as soon as we could and he'd see to it that they were up on lifts right away. He was as good as his word. We were on the road by noon.

Several hours behind the others, Nick and I lost even more time to confusing road signs in Pasco. After a stop for directions we resumed our ride east toward the towns of Prosser, Mabton, and eventually southeast across the brown and rolling Horse Heaven Hills to that day's scheduled lunch stop in Bickleton. We had already eaten, but stopped there anyway for a rest and some photos. Minutes after we pulled up in front of the Bluebird Café about a dozen bikes, all Triumphs, rolled up behind us.

It was a group on a guided tour out of British Columbia. Nick and I sat and talked with a couple from the Midlands in England as the tiny café filled with the smell of sweat-stained black leather and Cordura nylon, and someone punched up about five dollars' worth of insanely loud rock music on the jukebox. The tour group was very international, and varied greatly in age and background. They were unanimous on one thing—they were having a blast. They'd left B.C. several days earlier and were headed for San Francisco. Two of them had put diesel in their Triumphs by mistake, and even they were having a ball riding in the chase truck towing their ailing bikes.

Nick and I reluctantly took our leave and continued southwest toward what was probably the oddest stop on the ride. High atop a bluff on the north bank of the Columbia River near Maryhill is the Stonehenge Memorial, erected by a man named Sam Hill to honor the memory of local soldiers who died in the first world war. It's not an exact replica of the original in England, but more like what that one might have looked like when it was new, right out of the box. The setting is dusty, bare, and wind-whipped, and made me think not only about war and its consequences, but how much dirt I'd be coughing up later that evening.

We spent the night in a resort in North Bonneville. In the morning the Weather Channel gave us the bad news. Rain, and lots of it, right where we were headed—the Windy Ridge Viewpoint, which in good weather offers a harrowing close-up view of the aftermath of Mount St. Helens' most recent tantrum, followed by the Paradise Inn, more than 5000 feet up the side of Mount Rainier. The low, sullen clouds started leaking an hour into the ride. By lunch in Randle I was soaked from my neck to my knees, but very glad to be on the Wing with its barn-door fairing and wide windscreen. By about halfway up Mount Rainier I'd have traded it for a canoe. It was the first rain on the mountain for months, and it was making up for it all at once. Trees fell, mud slid, streams overflowed their banks. The raindrops sounded like buckshot on my helmet. By the time we floated into the parking lot of the Inn, all the roads on the mountain had been closed.

The road crews worked through the night to re-open them, and in the morning we upped anchor and sloshed down the mountain in a steady, heavy rain that occasionally let up just long enough to fool us into thinking the worst was over before opening up on us again. Rain means no photos, but take my word for it, the volcano region is spectacular. I'd been there years ago and always wanted to come back, just not under these circumstances.

By midday we were all so cold and wet there was no point in worrying about it any more, and we started enjoying the ride again. We stopped for wonderfully greasy cheeseburgers at a place in Greenwater where Nick, through a slip of the tongue during a conversation about low-light photography, earned himself the unfortunate nickname The Flashing Dutchman. Lucky for him the ride was almost over, or we'd have worn that joke down to the cord. The rain slacked off, then stopped. After a final photo op at Snoqualmie Falls, we returned the rental bikes and were driven to a hotel by the airport from which we'd all depart in the morning.

So, how good an idea was it for the Washington tourism people to invite a bunch of motojournalists to ride around the state? It's been weeks since I got home, and I still have this mental picture of rolling hills and deep blue water and the wide Columbia that I can't get out of my head. Sometimes I swear the wind is laden with the scent of golden grasslands, or the murmur of a rocky stream. In the distance I imagine the dim outline of a conical mountain through the fog, or what looks like a farmhouse shrouded in morning mist.

If you ask me, it was a *great* idea.

Why Are Motorcycles
So Hard To Work On?

(TREAD LIFE, 2009)

I drove into town this afternoon to the Honda shop to pick up a bottle of coolant so I can finally put the V-Strom back together after the Great Valve-Adjustment Fiasco of '09. While I was there I went around back to talk to the mechanic, who has done all of the work on my bike that I haven't done myself, despite him working for a Honda shop and me riding a Suzuki.

He was sitting on a stool beside a lift on which sat the filthiest old quad I've ever seen. There was so much mud caked on it I wasn't sure what brand of quad it was. I joked that it was nice when the customers cleaned their bikes before they brought them in for service. He said this one wasn't bad, and I should see one of the really dirty ones.

I congratulated him on having the patience to sit there all day and work on mutts like that quad, because it had taken me three weeks just to adjust the valves on the V-Strom. He knows me well enough to realize

I wasn't talking about three weeks of eight-hour days, but rather an hour here and an hour there, often with several days between those hours to wait for parts or let my aching knees and back recover.

We got to talking about how hard it was to work on some bikes. I told him some of the horror stories the V-Strom valve adjust had generated, and he trumped every one with a tale of his own about newer Hondas, especially the sportbikes, some of which are so compact that you have to remove the injector bodies to adjust the valves.

On the drive home I thought about this, and wondered when and why motorcycles got so hard to work on. When I started riding, it seemed like you were practically expected to do your own maintenance. BMW motorcycles came with toolkits so complete you could almost strip the bike down to the bare frame by the side of the road. Even low-dollar Japanese bikes came with a little blue plastic bag crammed so full of tools you could never fit them all back inside once you took them out.

Now? Not so much. Some of the test bikes I've ridden in recent years came with a spark-plug wrench, a screwdriver, and three wrenches made of steel as hard as old cheese. Harleys, which for years had a reputation for stopping dead due to factors like a change in humidity, still don't come with tools of any kind.

All I can figure is the manufacturers don't want me messing with the bike at all. That's understandable, I guess, in the age of emissions standards and corporate liability, but dammit, if that's the way they want to play it, they ought to make sure every shop selling their brand employs mechanics who can use tools for something other than scratching their asses.

Some years back, I stopped by a Suzuki dealer to ask about a valve adjust on the bike I was riding at the time. The only guy in the shop looked about 20, and had on a T-shirt with the name of some heavy-metal band across the front. He was holding a torque wrench the way a monkey would hold a violin.

This did little to instill confidence in his mechanical ability. Still, I was already there, so I asked him if he'd ever done the valves on the model of bike I had, and he said, "No, but I've done the valves on my CBR600, and that's the same kind of valves, right? With the little round things?"

I thanked him for his time, rode away, and did the job myself. It only took me two weeks back then. I guess I'm slowing down in my old age.

Unpopular Opinions:
Sound? Off.

(TREAD LIFE, 2008)

Everyone is entitled to their own opinion, but not their own facts.
—Sen. Daniel Patrick Moynihan

Talking to motorcyclists about loud pipes is like bringing up the subject of gun control at an NRA meeting. The argument—not the discussion, mind you, but the argument—gets emotional before anyone has the chance to think calmly about the facts of the issue, if indeed anyone ever has.

It's worth noting that both motorcyclists and gun owners hotly defend their respective positions on the basis of personal freedom, a cherished American birthright, ride free or die, cold dead hands, blah blah blah.

Of the two groups, gun owners are on far more solid ground,

thanks to the Second Amendment, which—although grammatically tortuous and speckled with extra commas that still leave its original meaning open to interpretation—has withstood all attempts to neuter it.

The personal-freedom rationale for putting loud pipes on a motorcycle is hogwash. I can't find anything in the Constitution about the right to be a pain in the ass. Federal law prohibits fitting any non-approved exhaust system to a motorcycle that's ridden on the street. The only reason people get away with it so often is the U.S. has no national police force, and state and local law enforcement agencies have no authority to enforce federal laws. They can, however, issue citations for violations of state and local noise limits.

But as long as you're prudent with the throttle, you probably won't get caught. Many riders take this as permission to gut their pipes and ride loud and proud. They're not totally without shame, though, because they've come up with a noble-sounding justification for this: Loud pipes save lives.

The theory is that car drivers—you know, those goobers with the cell phones pasted to their ears, the screaming kids in the back seat, and the stereo turned up loud enough to shatter the windows—will hear motorcycles even if they don't see them, and not run them off the road while reaching into the backseat to give little Timmy a good smack.

The emotional appeal of this argument is undeniable. Most accidents involving a car and a bike turn out to be the car's fault. It's not unusual to hear of the car driver in such cases getting a small fine, and the bike rider needing years of physical therapy to walk again. All of us who ride have had days where it seemed like we had targets on our backs, and every car on the road had crosshairs for a hood ornament.

The problem is the claim that loud pipes saves lives doesn't hold water. There's no objective, peer-reviewed study that I'm aware of that shows they do, and no thinking person should be convinced by the hand-me-down evidence ("A friend of a friend says he knew a guy who...") loud-pipe advocates so often resort to.

It's also notoriously difficult to prove a negative. If something happens, like a car hitting a motorcycle, it's usually possible to work back from the point of impact, reconstruct the series of events that led up to it, and figure out why it happened.

But if an oncoming car fails to turn in front of you, what's the reason? What prevented that? Your headlight? Your brightly colored riding gear? Your loud pipes? The fact that the car driver was paying attention to traffic and saw you coming?

Another problem with depending on loud pipes for protection from cars is it relies on someone else—the driver—caring enough about your safety and well-being to react, and react properly, and react in time. By subscribing to the loud-pipe method of non-defensive driving, motorcyclists place their safety in the hands of the very people they don't trust not to run them off the road or turn in front of them, and who prompted them to buy loud pipes in the first place.

This passive strategy also assumes drivers are actually paying attention to the sounds outside their cars. Ask any firefighter or cop or paramedic how often cars fail to pull over to the curb in response to a fire truck or ambulance coming up behind them with the siren wailing and the light bar flashing. Do you really think a set of loud pipes is going to work any better?

Then there are the broader social issues. Loud pipes piss off non-riders. That's indisputable. And they're pissing off an increasing number of riders, too, who find their welcome less warm at events where the local cops conduct mass sound checks, corralling everything from Harleys with straight pipes to BMWs with catalytic converters; in urban areas where motorcyclists' downtown access is restricted to certain hours, or prohibited altogether; and in national parks where the only kind of rolling thunder anyone wants to hear precedes the storm blowing in off the mountain.

In response to some of the laws being contemplated to silence noisy motorcycles, bikers' rights groups, including the AMA, say it's unfair to target bikes when some trucks and buses make just as much, if not more, noise. They also point out that no one stops car drivers from installing non-compliant replacement mufflers and exhaust systems when the stock ones on their cars break or wear out.

But the non-riding public isn't complaining about trucks and buses as often as it is about motorcycles. And there aren't an awful lot of people putting straight pipes on 10-year-old Toyotas and then driving around town goosing the throttle at stoplights.

Is it fair to single out bikes? No. Is it happening anyway? Yes. Can "they" go ahead and pass laws against loud bikes—maybe against all motorcycles—if they want to? Yes. Is that fair? No.

So what do we do?

We start by getting real.

Let's say there are bears—big, hungry, vicious ones—in the city park. They shouldn't be there, maybe there's even a law against bears being in the park, but they're there anyway, and everybody knows it.

Now, anybody with a lick of sense will stay out of the park. Some people, however, will get all indignant about the situation, and puff up their chests and go marching into the park anyway, loudly insisting it's their right to do so. And they'll get eaten by the bears.

Just as there is sometimes a difference between what's legal and what's right, there's often a huge gap between the way the world is supposed to work and the way it really does. The trick is to recognize the difference, and act accordingly.

Whatever we motorcyclists do about loud pipes and the corrosive effect they have on the relationship between motorcyclists and the rest of society, we need to do it ourselves, and soon.

Because if we don't, the bears will do it for us.

Unpopular Opinions:
Be Careful What You Wish For

(TREAD LIFE, 2009)

Sometimes well-intentioned actions produce an outcome that's the opposite of what was originally intended, or they solve one problem while creating another that's just as bad. Let's say you drive a gas guzzler and you're feeling guilty about your contribution to global warming. So you sell the guzzler and buy a smaller, more fuel-efficient car.

But have you really made a difference? You sold your old car to someone who will go right on driving it, and you bought a new car to replace it. Now there are two cars on the road where there was only one to begin with. You haven't done anything to reduce global warming; if anything you've made it worse. All you've really done is sell your guilt.

You can see the potential for this sort of backfire in the effort to promote motorcycles as a viable transportation alternative, and convince people to leave their cars at home and ride bikes to work, to school, to the grocery store...well, maybe not the grocery store. As someone who didn't own or have access to a car for about a year back in the 1970s, I can tell you the number of round trips I had to make to Safeway on a CB500 Four just to keep the cupboards half full was more than enough to offset any savings on gas.

There are more good reasons why riding a bike instead of driving a car just doesn't pencil out. If the price of gas is putting a serious hurt on you, what do you think the monthly payments on a bike will do? Then there's riding gear—a helmet, a jacket and pants, gloves, boots—none of which you need in your car. Throw in another insurance policy, and the price of maintenance and tires, then factor in the number of days each year when it's too hot, too cold, or too wet to ride, or the task at hand demands a device with a trunk, seating for more than two, and some weather protection—days the motorcycle sits in the garage unused—and it's obvious why you're never going to get Mr. and Mrs. Suburbia to trade in the Tahoe for a couple of scooters.

But suppose they did, along with hundreds of thousands of other people, making one of the motorcycle industry's fondest wishes come true. That would be a good thing, right?

Wouldn't it?

More riders will inevitably result in more crashes and fatalities, no matter how well trained those riders are. That will attract the attention of legislators, regulators, insurers, a national media already convinced that motorcycles are death machines, and—you might want to send the children out of the room now—lawyers.

This will inevitably lead to more restrictive laws—mandatory DOT-approved fully armored protective jacket and pants laws, any-one?—more public backlash as a few bad apples suddenly become entire orchards of them, and in general the kind of governmental scrutiny on the local, state, and federal level that motorcycling has so far escaped by virtue of being too small an insect to bother swatting very hard.

Currently motorcyclists can argue that they should be exempt from emissions regulations because they constitute a small minority of road users. But if the number of bikes on the road gets high enough, that excuse won't fly. If you laughed when you saw the optional air bag on the latest Honda Gold Wing, you probably won't think it's very funny when it's a government-mandated requirement on your dual-sport, along with a roll cage, arm restraints, and any number of half-assed "safety" features thought up by know-nothing politicians.

The sad thing is I'm pretty sure I'll live long enough to see some of this stuff anyway. So why hurry it along? Next time someone asks you why you ride a motorcycle, tell them it's because you're too poor to afford a car. Don't let on how much you enjoy it. The longer we keep the secret, the longer the fun will last.

Northern Exposure

(RIDER, 1997)

The bickering couple seated to my left on the plane has lapsed into a tight-lipped silence. She's glowering at the back of the seat in front of her, and he's playing video games on a laptop. He's closed the window so he can see the screen better, so I miss seeing Anchorage from the air as we descend for landing. My first glimpse of it comes as I trudge through the airport: a wall of stark, snow-streaked mountains rising sharply toward a low, cloudy sky. It's the Fourth of July, summer in Alaska. It's raining.

The car from the Glacier Bear Inn bed and breakfast picks me up and takes me to my room, where I find it's the custom in many Alaskan houses to remove your shoes before entering. I put on my warmest socks and join my fellow tour members in the common room. There are just four others beside me. Jim and Janice Mulvaney from Denver, Jim Crocker from Fort Worth, and Jerry Holl from San Diego. The Mulvaneys and Crocker have been on Edelweiss Alps tours. Holl and I are rookies.

After the introductions it strikes me that there aren't enough names to go around. We have two Jerrys, two Jims, and a Janice—five names beginning with J. Also Keith Hull, our tour guide, and Keith, manager of the Glacier Bear. We have dinner that night at the Regal Alaska, a hotel on Spenard Lake. Along with adjoining Lake Hood, it's home base for the world's largest fleet of float planes, the only practical way to get in and out of the roadless bush country and the interior.

We assemble the next morning for the first of the briefings that take place each day over breakfast. Today we're riding to Seward, 120 miles southwest of Anchorage on Resurrection Bay. For part of the day we'll ride along Turnagain Arm, a body of water known for bore tides, extremely rapid inflows of water that can and do catch tourists off-guard and trap them in the quicksand-like mud. Keith warns us not to go walking on the mud flats. He drives the point home with a cautionary tale of a tourist who became mired and had to be pulled out by a rescue helicopter. "They got him halfway out," Keith says. "The top half."

The sky threatens rain as we leave the Glacier Bear. In addition to leading Edelweiss tours, Keith rents bikes. A few days before I arrived the BMW boxer I had asked for was totaled, so I'm offered a Kawasaki KLR650 with triple Givi hard bags or a BMW F650 with no bags and a mere 200 miles on the clock. I opt for the Kawasaki.

Our first taste of Alaska is a flock of Dall sheep cavorting on a sheer cliffside along Turnagain Arm. Traffic slows to watch, and the sheep appear to be hanging around for no other reason than to witness lumbering motorhomes swerving dangerously toward each other as their drivers crane their necks to make out the tiny white shapes hopping from crag to crag.

Jim and Janice have gone on ahead. Jim and Jerry and I take a side trip to the Alyeska Ski Lodge for a cup of coffee. Rain spits down

out of the gray sky as we pass the tiny town of Girdwood, which is revel-
ing in its annual Forest Fair. A sign by the entrance to the Fair grounds
says, "No dogs, no politicians, no religious orders." I order a blueberry
muffin and get something the size of a small birthday cake. It's unbeliev-
ably delicious.

Back on the road we buck strong headwinds howling up the Arm.
We take the road to Portage Glacier, only to find it's obscured by the
weather. The rain is bucketing down now. I put on my boot and glove
covers in the shelter of a closed rest room. Out in the water by the visi-
tor's center float fantastically shaped chunks of ice, pieces of the glacier
that have broken off and drifted away. Their cores are a startling shade
of deep blue. This is a characteristic of glacier ice, which is so dense it
absorbs all colors of the spectrum except blue, which it reflects. It's bluer
on cloudy days than on clear ones. It's very blue today.

The group, including Keith in the Edelweiss Suburban, loaded
with enough gear and food to provision a small army, and towing a four-
bike trailer with the F650 on it, meets at the Summit Lake Lodge for
lunch. We comment on the heavy traffic heading back toward Anchorage. Keith tells us Seward is a popular vacation town with folks in Anchorage. The procession of motorhomes and trailers is known to locals
along the way as "the 'Bago train." After the Fourth of July weekend,
traffic will decrease to a trickle. Lunch is prompt, good, and expensive
by southern standards. To an Alaskan, even a Connecticut Yankee is a
"southerner," as is everyone else who lives in the lower 48.

What has already come to be known as the 5-J Tour arrives in
Seward. An enormous cruise ship is docked in the harbor, towering over
the fishing and pleasure craft like a Sequoia in a cornfield. We check
into the Harborview Inn, a new and tidy motel a block from the waterfront. I experience an *X-Files* moment when I see that our hosts at the
Harborview are—Jerry and Jolene! Another Jerry! Two more J's!

On tonight's schedule is a picnic served by Keith in one of the pavilions along Resurrection Bay, from which an astonished fisherman hauled a 340-pound halibut the day before. Keith's resumé includes a stint in the food-service industry. That industry's loss is our considerable gain. His definition of "picnic" includes grilled halibut, barbecued chicken, cole slaw, potato salad, fruit, chips, drinks, and pie for dessert. The award for the hands-down, shoot-potato-salad-out-your-nose-funniest story of the day goes to Jim and Janice who, riding double, pulled up to the ticket booth at Exit Glacier north of town and were asked by the ranger, "Are you two together?"

At 11:30 that night, the streets of Seward are deserted. Despite overcast skies, it's still light enough outside to read a newspaper. Time seems unreal, like foreign money when you travel overseas: It isn't green, it has pictures of dead royalty or obscure landmarks on it, and it's hard to take seriously, like Monopoly money. Maybe it's a problem with the hour-exchange rate—the hands on my watch keep moving, but it's just not getting darker. Maybe we're on metric time. All I know is I can't get to sleep, and when I finally do it's time to get up.

A free day in Seward. Jerry Holl and the Mulvaneys ride to Homer and back, a round trip of about 340 miles. Jim Crocker and Keith and I explore some of the back roads around town, some paved, some not. Keith leads the way to the far side of Resurrection Bay. Looking across the water at the town, the cruise ship looks like a toy. The mountains that ring the bay loom large and ominous. They're imposing as hell, obviously designed from the git-go to be all mountain, with none of that wimpy hill stuff leading up to the steep parts. They make the mountains around my house back home look like speed bumps.

We turn on a side road and see a building that resembles one of several Princess Resort Hotels in Alaska. It's new, and has a bright blue roof, lots of windows, and what appears to be a penthouse restaurant atop a tower. It is in fact a guard tower, and the building is not a resort hotel, but the new Spring Creek State Prison. I'm informed of this by an armed guard in a light-barred Bronco who intercepts me in the parking lot. I play dumb tourist—not much of a stretch under the circumstances—and he tells me indulgently that this really isn't a good place to stop and take pictures. We leave with the distinction of being the only people ever to get thrown out of jail in Seward.

We seek tamer amusement at Exit Glacier. A short hike brings us to the face of the glacier itself, a river of ice flowing out of the 300-square-mile Harding Ice Field, from which eight glaciers reach the sea. Deep blue glacier ice is visible in the cracks. Signs warn hikers to keep back, as huge chunks weighing tons can break off at any moment. Tourists being what they are, several are standing under wide overhangs, slapping the ice and grinning for friends with cameras, while others climb above them and leap over crevasses 10 feet deep.

We walk back to the bikes, passing hikers wearing bear bells, jingling merrily. The bells are supposed to alert bears and scare them off. It reminds me of when I was a kid, and bells heralded the approach of the ice cream truck. I mention this to Keith, who says they sometimes find bear bells in the stomachs of "nuisance bears" killed by rangers. A stuffed wolverine at an interpretive center reminds Keith of a friend's assessment of that animal's temperament: "If wolverines weighed a hundred pounds I'd never go into the forest."

The KLR is working out better than I had expected. During an exploration of a dirt road it skips over potholes like a dancer. Jim's BMW twin skitters like a dowager trying to keep the mud off her opera slippers. The rain gets worse, so we leave the bikes and our soggy raingear at the motel, pile into the Suburban, and warm up in an old church converted to a coffee house. Van Morrison and the Chieftains are playing on the stereo. The locals do their polite best to ignore us, and we do our best to blend in. Next we visit the Alaska Sealife Center, where I'm suddenly 12 years old, with my nose pressed up against the underwater viewing windows in the seal tanks, and taking picture after picture of the comical puffins splashing and diving.

The next day we saddle up and head for Sheep Mountain, 247 miles from Seward, backtracking along Turnagain Arm. The wind is sharp and cold. The sleepless nights and unrelenting headwinds are wearing me down. Through Anchorage and heading north, the KLR is out of its element on the 65-mph four-lane highway, and it's a toss-up whether duct tape on the frame rails would be more comfortable than the narrow seat. Over lunch in Palmer I announce my intention to switch to the F650, despite its lack of bags. The others immediately offer tank bags, rain covers, bungee nets. Are these guys pals or what?

At Sheep Mountain Lodge we sleep in bunkhouses, two to a room. A large contingent of touring bicyclists has arrived, and the management has churlishly bumped us from the private cabins Keith had booked. At breakfast the two groups steal surreptitious glances at each other's outlandish outfits, like caravan travelers meeting at a desert oasis, shy but curious.

Today it's Sheep Mountain to Fairbanks. Jim Crocker sees a small animal that becomes known as the Mysterious Furry Critter of the Frozen North. I spot my first moose, grazing in the water by the side of the road. Later I see a beautiful speckled grouse-like bird, a ptarmigan. It leaps in front of my bike and ricochets off the F650's front fender with a sickening thump. I mention this to Keith at lunch in Paxson, at the east end of the Denali Highway. He tells me the ptarmigan is the state bird. Great. I'm here three days and I whack the state bird. Maybe I'll get into Spring Creek after all.

We ride west on the Denali Highway until the pavement runs out around mile marker 20, then return to the main road. The side trip rewards us with glaciers and towering crags we would not have otherwise seen. The stretch of road between Paxson and Delta Junction and over Isabel Pass is simply stunning, spectacular, magnificent—pick your favorite travel writer's cliché, then multiply it by about 12.

We parallel the Trans-Alaska Pipeline. At a construction zone we stop while graders push gravel and dirt around. I chat with the worker holding the stop/slow sign. He moved to Alaska from Oregon 26 years ago. I mention I live in Oregon. He bets me I've never heard of the little town he's from, and names it. The hell I haven't, I say, and to his astonishment tell him exactly where it is. Later that day I meet another Oregonian, this one from Tillamook. Who's back home, minding the store?

This is the longest travel day, 340 miles. I pause to gas up and grab a bite at Delta Junction before tackling the last 100 miles to Fairbanks. The sun comes out at last, while the weather to the south looks ominous. A miles-wide cloud trailing tendrils of rain drifts across the sky like a gigantic jellyfish. Nine hours after leaving Sheep Mountain I arrive in Fairbanks, 20 minutes behind the others, dog-tired.

Keith has a special genius for arranging unique lodging and meals. We stay in cabins on the Chena River, and dine on all-you-can-eat salmon, halibut, and ribs at Alaskaland, a tacky but entertaining theme park (suggested motto: "Admission is free, and worth every penny!"). A cloudburst drives us into a dining hall with a metal roof where the pounding rain makes conversation nearly impossible. Two of Keith's bike renters join us, a father and son from Georgia. They're bound for the top of the pipeline, at Prudhoe Bay on the Arctic Ocean.

After breakfast the next morning we visit the museum at the University of Alaska at Fairbanks, and make another pass through Alaskaland before leaving town. The flight museum there features complete aircraft, as well as partial aircraft apparently recovered from crash sites.

A massive 16-cylinder radial engine is missing several cylinders, the bent stumps of broken con rods poking up through the crankcase testifying to the violence with which they were removed. I've seen museums dedicated to flight before, but never one that so emphatically demonstrates the consequences of failing to maintain flight.

On the way to Denali National Park, we pass a tavern called Skinny Dick's Halfway Inn. The walls and ceiling are covered with bills, mostly singles and a few fives, stapled there by travelers, ostensibly for Dick's retirement. The inscriptions on some of the bills would make a sailor blush—I can only imagine the effect on the economy if they're ever put into general circulation. Skinny Dick himself is behind the bar. "Has the conversation gotten around to sex yet," he pipes in a raspy voice, "or are we still talkin' about the weather?"

Lunch at the Depot Cafe in Nenana. The TV by the pool table reports a 6.4 earthquake yesterday, centered about 125 miles southwest of Anchorage. Jim Crocker, a Texas native, says almost wistfully that he's never been in an earthquake. Keith, Jerry, and I, who all have, assure him he's not missing anything.

The wind is tossing the F650 around like a kitten with a ball of string. From the front, then one side, then the other, but never from behind, which is the only direction I wouldn't mind. After about 40 miles of this I see a sign that says WIND. If that wasn't wind all along back there, what the hell was it? And how much worse can it get? My answer comes in the form of a bright orange wind sock, placed mid-span on a bridge over a river. It's sticking straight out sideways like a traffic cone.

My cabin is on the glacier-fed Nenana River. We have a free day tomorrow, and this is the perfect place to spend it relaxing. No TV in the room, no phone. I go to the gift shop for a book. Amid the Grishams and Kings and Clancys I find two true classics of the north, Jack London's *White Fang* and *Call of the Wild*, both in one volume.

Jim, Jim and Janice, and Jerry go flight-seeing over Denali Park. I'm not fond of airplanes to begin with, and the smaller the plane the less I like it. Or maybe I'm still thinking of the flight museum at Alaskaland. Anyway, I stay behind and read. Keith whips up another picnic on the deck by the river that evening, and we finish it off by passing around a book of poems by Robert Service and reading them out loud.

A free day in Denali. The lack of sleep finally catches up to me, and I feel as bad as I've ever felt without actually getting sick. I go back to bed after breakfast, wake up five hours later feeling better, and spend the rest of the afternoon loafing. Around four I ride into Denali Park to catch a glimpse of Mount McKinley, which the native Alaskans call Denali, the Great One. Measuring from its base, it's taller than Mount Everest, which sits on a plateau. McKinley rises 20,320 feet from an elevation of only 2,000 feet. But the mountain isn't "out" today, and is instead wreathed in clouds, which is the case two days out of three.

Jim's Mysterious Furry Critter of the Frozen North is spotted again, under an outhouse on the road into Denali Park, and is positively identified as a hoary marmot. That evening I spot my second, third, and fourth moose, a female and two youngsters, in the trees beside the hotel parking lot. Peering at them through the dense brush, what I initially take for saplings are in fact the female's hind legs—her heinie must be six feet off the ground. I approach to within 10 feet to snap pictures. Keith creeps up behind me and whispers, "If she flattens her ears, run like hell." Which way? I ask. "Just follow me," he says, then adds, "but don't get ahead of me."

The final day of the tour takes us from Denali back to Anchorage. It's bitterly cold and raining, and when it's not raining the clouds are so low I feel like I can stand up on the footpegs and touch them. Despite the weather, Jim and Jerry and I stop at the Talkeetna Moose Dropping Festival. This event does not, as a group of particularly humorless animal rights activists are rumored to have believed, involve dropping moose, but rather the droppings of moose. The end-product of moose digestion is incorporated into jewelry and used in contests of skill, and lends it name to various chocolate confections.

As we arrive, the Anchorage Scottish Pipe Band strikes up "Scotland the Brave." We lunch at the Roadhouse, where we are served by one of the top 10 friendliest waitresses in North America (the other nine are in Alaska, too) and watch locals mixing with out-of-towners who wouldn't ordinarily be caught dead at such a rube-fest and are trying hard not to let on how much fun they're having. I pose for a picture with a reindeer, which responds to the touch of my hand on its bristly coat by urinating in a splashing torrent. Add one more item to the list of liquids that won't soak through Gore-Tex. People in colorful costumes roam the tiny town, and I see more mixed-breed dogs than I've ever seen in one place outside the animal shelter. Another hour and a half on the road and we're back at the Glacier Bear, from which we'll catch rides to the airport and home in the morning.

Human habitation has a way of taming a place, of softening it, civilizing it. There are only a little over half a million people in Alaska, and they haven't even begun to take the rough edges off it. Maybe they never will. Maybe they just can't. If Montana is Big Sky country, Alaska is Big Everything country. The state motto should be, "There's nothing small here." Words are inadequate to express the sheer size and scope of the place—lakes miles long, mountains miles high, wooded hills rolling to the horizon in all directions.

See it while you still can, big, wild, empty Alaska, full of sights that'll make your brain doubt your eyes. See it on a motorcycle. And see it soon, before somebody gets to work on those rough edges.

Rescue Bikes

(1999)

We have two dogs, a three-year-old Golden Retriever named Winzer, and an eight-year-old Collie named Dancer, who is a rescue dog. She's not a rescue dog as in "Timmy's down the well, go get help," although if Timmy had treats in his pocket she'd dive in after him. In the dog world, a "rescue" is taking in a dog that's been abandoned or abused, with the object of finding it a good home. We originally took in Dancer "just for the weekend" until a permanent home came along. Right. Uh huh. There are now two leashes hanging on hooks by the front door, and two bowls on the kitchen floor.

Dog rescue has its counterpart in motorcycling. It works pretty much the same way, too. You hear about a bike that's been sitting neglected in a garage for years. Or one that's being ridden by some meathead who thinks adding oil is as good as changing it regularly. Or you're riding along and you spot a rusty front wheel sticking out from under a dirty tarp in a back yard. And *wham*—you're hooked. It's every bit as

effective as a pair of soulful brown eyes looking up at you, silently plead-
ing, "Pleeease, take me home!"

Some rescue dogs come in pretty bad shape, just like some rescue
bikes. Both will usually respond wonderfully to large doses of TLC. The
bikes don't express it so obviously, but you can almost feel the gratitude
as you lever off those bald tires, drain that oily sludge out of the forks,
sand down and primer those ugly spots of mange on the tank, and hook
up a fresh battery.

The hardest part of any rescue is giving up the rescuee to a good
home. That's why some people end up living in houses that seem to be
carpeted with dogs. (This is called "failing at rescue.") It's no different with motorcycles, especially if you're into one particular make and
model. I know a guy who has a garage piled high with Kawasaki triples
of all years and sizes, and a mini-store across town so crammed with
spare parts and new old stock that it's perilously close to exploding and
raining shards of seized H1 crankshafts and rusty gas tanks all over the
time zone. When you've gone this far down the path of madness, what's
another few yards?

Most rescue dogs have great untapped reserves of affection and
loyalty that they'll lavish on anyone who treats them with love and respect. Like their canine counterparts, rescue bikes often turn out to be
fiercely loyal companions whose company you miss long after they've
gone off to the Big Boneyard In The Sky.

I once bought a mongrel CB550 from the service manager of a
Honda shop. He had rescued it a piece at a time out of wrecked bikes
that passed through the shop on their way to the local salvage yards. It
had the K-model engine and carbs, the F-model airbox and pipes, and
sun- or fire-damaged instruments whose melted and drooping faces appeared to have been copied from a Salvador Dali painting. It looked like
it had been painted with a mop and a bucket, ran like a Swiss watch,

and idled so quietly you could hear each link of the cam chain roll off the cam sprocket. I rode that old dog everywhere, and sold it 14 years ago, but I can still see every dent and rust pock in its homely mug when I close my eyes.

Another time I got a call from a friend who said he'd spotted a mint Yamaha SR500 in a BMW shop. The shop had taken it in trade for a box of parts somebody needed to restore an old Boxer. The SR had been sitting in the corner of the showroom for a couple of weeks like an awkward party guest being ignored by haughty Beemerphiles. The clock showed 750 miles, the word "mint" was no exaggeration—it even had the scary OE tires—and to me it was every bit as much a purebred as any bike in the place. They were glad to get rid of it, and at the asking price of $750, this was less a rescue on my part than it was a theft that involved paperwork.

A few years later I learned of an '82 CBX at Honda's old facility in Gardena. It had been ridden hard and put away wet by a district rep, then given to the service department to train rookie mechanics, and finally parked at the end of a row of beater ATVs and power products in the back of a warehouse. I bought it for $2000, aired up the tires and charged the battery, and it fired right up. There literally was not room in my tiny garage for the SR alongside the six-cylinder CBX, so I reluctantly gave the Yamaha up to a good home.

The CBX was followed by an abused and neglected GS850 that became a magazine project bike. Soon after, however, it took ill with scary deep-engine noises. It would have cost more to fix it than I had into it, so I unbolted all the accessories, sold it as a fixer-upper, and bought the first new bike I'd owned in about 10 years, a '92 Honda CB750 Nighthawk.

Even this was a rescue of sorts. It had been sitting on the showroom floor for two years, and the shop was desperate to get rid of it. I asked how desperate, exactly. The salesman said, "Four grand, out the door." I took out the MasterCard I saved for emergencies like leaking roofs and said, "Sold."

Today our house has all the dogs it needs—or can stand. Of course, I say this knowing full well that any day now some throwaway dog could steal my heart, and there'll be another bowl on the kitchen floor. The same goes for rescue bikes. Lately the Nighthawk looks kind of lonely out there in the garage all by itself. Maybe it needs a playmate—a frisky little sportbike, say, or a big friendly sport-tourer....

Hey, what's that under the tarp over there? Here, boy!

Leap of F#&%!

(TREAD LIFE, 2009)

I wrote a while back about smells, and how they can conjure up memories of places you thought you'd forgotten. Tonight, I heard a sound that did the same thing.

I was watching *Masterpiece* on PBS's website. The current series is about Inspector Robbie Lewis, who in an earlier series—and a series of books before that—was the sidekick of Inspector Morse, an Oxford, England, police detective created by Colin Dexter.

At the end of the episode, when Lewis and his sergeant had unraveled a murder so convoluted that I gave up trying to figure out whodunit and just went along for the ride, the uniformed coppers arrived to cart off the guilty party. They put her in a police car, and as they were doing it, an extra walked through the foreground of the scene, wearing a yellow jacket and a flip-up motorcycle helmet. In the final scene this extra rode off on a police version of the Honda ST1100, which is called the Pan European over there.

In a lot of movies and TV shows I've seen that have motorcycles in them, they often add the sound of the bike later—and they often get it wrong, either by not bothering to match the rise and fall of the engine revs to the scene, or by making everything from two-stroke 125s to four-cylinder sportbikes sound like Harleys with straight pipes.

This time they got it right. I heard the unmistakable whir of the engine as the starter turned it over, the quavering idle, and the staggered power pulses of the V-four engine pushing gas through the stock exhaust, and bingo, there I was aboard my old ST1100 again.

I've been thinking about that bike a lot lately. I did a lot of fun stuff on it, and had a scary experience that was almost the last experience I ever had.

I was riding north through Tacoma, Washington, on Interstate 5 near the Tacoma Dome in heavy traffic. I was in the hot lane, and some joker in a Dodge pickup was right on my ass. We were going maybe 75, and I was too close to the car ahead for comfort, so I glanced over my right shoulder at the number two lane, saw it was clear, and signaled to change lanes. As I leaned the bike into the open spot, I turned my head forward again and looked at the car ahead of me, and out from under it, as if on a conveyor belt, came a four-by-four wooden post sitting in the middle of the lane, perpendicular to my path.

I yanked the handlebar as hard as I could, steering left to try to get as upright as possible before I hit the post. There was an almighty *whack* that nearly wrenched the grips from my hands as the ST smacked the post and took off like a 600-pound gooney bird, first the front end and then the back; at about the same time my butt and the seat parted ways; for a harrowing second or two the bike and I were pretty much flying above I-5 at an altitude of about two feet; and then the bike came back down with a thud like a dumpster full of doorknobs, still going at least 65, and the front wheel almost shook itself off the bike.

I assume some of the drivers around me saw what had happened and reacted quickly enough to give me room; all I remember is bulldogging the bike across two more lanes of traffic and onto the shoulder. The front rim was bent, but miraculously, the tire had held air. If the rim had bent enough to break the bead, I would never have made to the shoulder. There's no doubt in my mind that if I'd gone down in traffic that heavy I'd have been reduced to a paste by the time anyone stopped to see what they had run over.

That could be why ST1100s continue to appeal to me; you come through something like that without a scratch and you develop a great deal of respect for the bike you did it on.

I sold mine because my wrists would no longer tolerate the weight the riding position put on them. I know if I got another one I probably wouldn't ride it enough to justify the purchase.

But I have a feeling that if I ever needed a bike that would get me where I was going come hell, high water, or posts in the road, an ST1100 would be my first choice.

Volcano Tour

Visiting three of the Northwest's biggest hotheads

(AMERICAN RIDER)

I've never had an out-of-body experience, but here I am having an out-of-breath one. We're several thousand feet above sea level, high enough that my respiratory system's jetting is dangerously lean. On top of that I'm horsing a low-slung Heritage Softail from corner to corner on a road built like a snake's back—narrow, serpentine, and curving smoothly from crown to shoulder until it simply rolls out of sight into the valley below. The concept of guardrails, or even curbs, has yet to be embraced in this part of Washington state.

I'm following three guys on Honda ST1100 sport-tourers, which look like sleek black dolphins. Joe, Randy, and John are members of a loose confederation of self-medicating lunatics whose particular passion is long-distance, or LD, riding. An LD rider's idea of a laid-back weekend is riding a thousand miles in 24 hours, catching a few hours sleep, and doing it again. The Iron Butt Rally—a scavenger-hunt/sleep-deprivation experiment that can cover more than 11,000 miles in 11 days—is their World Series, their Super Bowl, and they crave a place on the starting line the way pilgrims yearn for paradise.

LD riders are nuts by pretty much anyone's definition. As a group they're also some of the nicest folks I've ever met. They don't give a bent spoke what you ride, only that you *do* ride. In June I attended an annual LD gathering at a restaurant in Kirkland, Washington, and Joe offered to show me three of the Northwest's volcanoes—Mount Rainier, Mount St. Helens, and Mount Hood—on my ride back home. Randy signed up for part of the trip—work beckoned Monday morning—and John would stay with Joe and me until White Salmon, on the north bank of the Columbia River. Joe and I would press on and spend the night at the Timberline Lodge on the slopes of Mount Hood.

Sunday morning we met at Randy's house east of Kirkland. Maps were spread out over seats, routes debated and rated for the interest factor of the road and the scenery, and a plan was settled on. We set out on Route 203, which led us through farmland still wet with morning dew. There's no smell like the smell of farm country in the morning, and even the smells that'd make you go *phew* later in the day make you glad to be alive. The Softail grumbled along happily, in its element on the gently curving roads.

The first scenic stop was Snoqualmie Falls. Like many natural wonders in the Northwest, the 270-foot-high falls were for centuries, and still are, sacred to local native tribes. They called it a "place of power," a name that came back to haunt them since there are now two electric power plants there, built by people who would be outraged if the Snoqualmies moved a lot of generators into the local church and fired them up. Within walking distance of the falls is a park with picnic tables and

an observation deck, and the Salish Lodge. Nearby there's fishing, skiing, and a diesel-powered railroad line operated by the Puget Sound
Railway Historical Association.

As we walked up the path to the observation deck, the roar of
the falls became louder. A thick mist hung in the air—so thick, in fact,
that the roar was all we got. Well, that, and wet. The falls, though right
in front of us, were completely obscured. We trudged back down to the
parking lot wiping off our glasses. "At least it *sounded* scenic," someone
said.

We left Route 203 and took a short hop on 18 to 169 and the town
of Enumclaw, our first gas stop. After gassing the Softail I went into the
station to shop for road food. There I found a member of our party, who
shall remain nameless, breakfasting on turkey jerky and a cherry Coke.
All that menu needed was a cigar to be a completely unbalanced meal. I
picked out a sandwich and some fruit and stowed them in the saddlebags
for later.

South of town we took Route 410, heading for Mount Rainier.
The route up to now had followed farm roads, straight for the most part,
bordered by neat little fields and pastures. Now the road began to climb
swiftly, and grew curvier by the mile. The Softail didn't mind the elevation change, but—lifelong sea-level dweller that I am—I did. At photo
stops I found myself gulping air and yawning.

Randy had planned a side trip up to Sunrise where a spectacular
view of Rainier awaited. But the road was closed by snow, still thick on
the ground in early June. While Randy conferred with park rangers
about an alternate route, Joe sidled across the road to a shaded hillside,
scooped up a handful of snow, and packed it into a neat round ball so
quickly there was no escaping the impression it was something he did often and well. Just as deftly he palmed it and stood patiently by the bikes
until Randy came out of the ranger station.

Moments later, after shaking the snow off his shoulders, Randy announced Plan B. We continued on along Route 410 to 123, and from there to 706, which skirts the southern slope of Rainier. Closed in winter, little-used—and apparently seldom repaired—in the summer, the pavement grew choppy. I struggled to keep pace with the others—did I mention these guys ride everywhere as if the hounds of hell were snapping at their heels?—and thought dark thoughts about whoever put the "soft" in Softail. Short-travel suspension, very limited cornering clearance, and a good-but-overworked single disc brake had me longing for those laid-back farm roads we'd started out on.

We rode through a landscape that looked almost alpine, if not lunar. On one side of the road was a sheer rock wall, on the other a sheer drop-off. Swiftly flowing rivulets of water cascaded from above, and trickled down the wet walls of tunnels hewn from solid rock. A sign that said "Avalanche Area" made me grateful the Softail's pipes were no more thunderous than they were. Our destination was the Paradise Inn, which we hoped would afford us the view we'd been denied at Sunrise.

They say the metaphorical road to paradise is a rough one. The earthly one made what had come before seem like an interstate. As we parked and shucked out of our riding gear I spotted a very low, very custom Softail parked nearby. However bad it had been for me, it had to have been worse for that guy. We burgered up at the Paradise Inn and soaked up the breathtaking—literally for me—view of Mount Rainier right out the lodge window. The Inn is the hub of a network of hiking trails in the summer and, with an annual average snowfall of 630 inches, a skier's paradise in winter. A scale model of Mount Rainier National Park showed us at a glance where we'd been, and where we were going.

Back on the road, another waterfall lay along our path, Narada Falls, on the Paradise River. The 168-foot cataract is three feet higher than Niagara. A steep path led 200 feet down to the bottom. I passed on a photo op, convinced I'd need bottled oxygen to make it back up. Randy graciously offered to make the trek and take my camera with him. Joe, who was organizing a rally in which Randy was entered, and was secretly using our ride to scout possible bonus locations, decided on the spot to make a photo of the falls taken from the bottom of the path a points-paying bonus. He chuckled as Randy went off down the path. "I hope you enjoy the climb," he said quietly, "because you'll be making it again in August."

Next came a long loop, Route 706 east to Elbe, then 7 south to Morton, and 12 east to Randle where at least two dozen late-model sportbikes sat clustered around the pumps at the gas station and store. I had become accustomed to being the only Harley rider in our little group. Suddenly the group I was the only Harley rider in got bigger. The cool air of the higher elevations was gone, replaced by a baking heat. I bought a couple of bottles of water, refilled the Camelbak in my jacket pocket, and we headed south out of Randle toward Mount St. Helens on a series of forest routes.

The less said about those roads the better. Tight, bumpy, and often simply disappearing at the edges, they kept my attention riveted on the pavement instead of the landscape. Vestiges of the devastation of the 1980 eruption weren't as obvious as I'd thought they'd be, until we pulled off at a scenic overlook. We were looking at the peak from pretty much the same angle as the camera that had taken the now-familiar footage of the explosion and collapse of the mountain. A huge scooped-out section, filled with dirty snow, was all that was left of the top 1300 feet of the mountain. Rank upon rank of dead trees still lay on the slopes like wet hair plastered on a skull. Later I learned Mount St. Helens is still active, and is building another dome inside the crater.

Randy had to be at work the next day, so he said goodbye and rode home. Joe, John, and I pressed on south toward the Columbia River on a series of forest routes, guided primarily by the on-board global positioning satellite receivers—gadgets beloved of LD riders—mounted on their bikes. Afterward, even with the help of a detailed road atlas, I could barely find most of the roads we took—they're represented by tiny wiggly lines that might easily be stray dog hairs that fell on the map, and they didn't seem much wider than that while we were on them. If I had it to do over again, especially if I was doing it over again on a Softail, I'd probably wuss out and take Route 504 from the Mount St. Helens area over to I-5 and from there to 14, along the north bank of the Columbia.

After a wrong turn and a backtrack we found the route to the Columbia River. John, who lives in White Salmon, Washington, accompanied us across the Columbia to Hood River, Oregon, and a restaurant he likes there. Tired and sore and smelling the barn, I got careless and made the mistake of hitting the bridge spanning the river leaned over and on the gas, only to find out it was a steel-grate bridge, a type that does not typically reward such antics. Coffee with my meal would have been redundant—my heart didn't stop pumping wildly for an hour. After dinner Joe and I left John and headed south through Oregon on Highway 35 to the Timberline Lodge on the slopes of the day's third volcano, Mount Hood.

The Timberline was built in 1937 by the Works Progress Administration out of huge timbers and native stone. The word "magnificent" is inadequate to describe the place. At 6000 feet, some of the best skiing in Oregon is literally on your doorstep, and when Joe and I checked in that evening in early June, the slopes were open—not that either of us wanted anything but a stop at the bar and a good night's sleep. Only Joe got the latter, as the elevation broke my night into a series of short, breathless naps.

Later than we'd planned the next morning we had breakfast in the Lodge and said our goodbyes. Joe headed back home to Seattle and I pointed the Softail's front wheel toward the Oregon coast. Mount Hood loomed in my rear-view mirrors for a long while, and finally slid behind the trees. Soon I was back on farm roads, where both the Softail and I breathed much easier.

Museum Of The Mind

(TREAD LIFE, 2008)

I read yesterday that publisher Source Interlink has axed *Motorcyclist Retro*, which was edited by Mitch Boehm, who I worked with at *Motorcyclist* for the first six months of 1988 before I fled L.A. for the bucolic splendor of Oregon.

I'm sorry to see the title go, even though only a handful of issues were produced. I like reading about old motorcycles despite having little interest in owning or riding them. I used to own a very nice '75 Honda CB400F that I got while I worked at *Cycle Guide*. We had run an article on a couple of Honda 400s—a Japan-only 400cc four-cylinder with a trick valve train not unlike today's VTEC, and a three-cylinder two-stroke decked out in Rothman's livery—and a sidebar about the editor's own '70s-vintage CB400F, which he named Precious.

The sidebar prompted a letter (no email in those days) to the magazine from a reader who said he had six—that's right, six—CB400Fs in his garage, none of which had more than 1100 miles on the clock. He had bought his first one in 1975, the first year of production, and loved it. Not long after that, someone told him Honda wasn't going to make any more of them after that year. So he did what anyone would do—he went back to the dealer and bought five more.

Sitting in my office at *Cycle Guide*, reading this letter, I had to wonder if the guy was putting us on. Then I got to the good part. He was willing to sell his bikes for $500 each. He said they were in pristine condition. All we had to do was come and get them.

At the time I had no history with CB400Fs. I had owned a CB500F and a CB550F years before, and they were competent if dull machines. I'd never ridden a CB400F, but I'd heard other people talking about them as if they were something special. That pretty much convinced me I had to have one. Mark Twain had a phrase for it—getting drunk on the smell of somebody else's cork.

As it happens I grew up in the San Francisco Bay Area, where the man lived. It was December, and I had plans to drive north to visit my parents for the holidays. I finagled the *Cycle Guide* van for the trip, took $1000 out of savings—to buy one for me, and one for a buddy—and hit the road.

When I got to the man's house and he opened the garage door, I was amazed. Every word of what he'd written was true. I stood there looking at a row of CB400Fs—five red ones and a blue one—each one absolutely showroom fresh. I walked down the row checking the odometers. The highest mileage on any of them was 1111.

The man explained that he used to ride them all once a week to keep the batteries charged, but as he got older this became more of a chore than he cared for, hence the decision to sell them. The sidebar had given him the impression that among the staff of *Cycle Guide* might be one or two enthusiasts who'd appreciate these bikes.

I appreciated two of them, a red one for me and a blue one for my buddy, into the back of the van, handed over $1000 in cash, and grinned like a Cheshire cat all the way back to L.A.

Some people who buy vintage and classic bikes pamper them like Faberge eggs. I'm not one of those people. If I can't ride a motorcycle I don't see the point of owning it. And that's where I began to see the flaw in my plan.

First, the little 400F was, as advertised, pristine. The problem was the real world was anything but pristine. For every hour I rode the bike I spent another hour cleaning it. That got old fast, but I wanted to protect my investment. The only other option was to build a museum and put it behind velvet ropes. But my house was barely big enough for its human occupants, never mind moving the inhabitants of the garage inside.

The second problem was how far motorcycles had come in the 12 years since the 400F was made. It just wasn't much fun to ride. I had to wring its neck to get anything like decent acceleration out of it, and the brakes and handling weren't up to the cut-and-thrust of city traffic, never mind L.A. freeways.

I brought the bike with me to Oregon in 1988, and rode it now and then. But the winters up here are long and wet, and it spent most of its time in the basement. I finally took the battery out, drained the gas tank, drained the engine oil and replaced it with fresh oil, and threw a sheet over it. That's where it stayed until I sold it to a motorcycle magazine editor a few years ago.

Even though I never had much fun riding it, I always enjoyed looking at it. Some days I'd go down to the basement, take the sheet off, and sit on it. It was a beautiful little bike, as cute as a puppy, and reminded me of good times in a warm, sunny place.

And that's why I'm so sorry to see *Motorcyclist Retro* go away. In four decades of riding that includes working at three national motorcycle magazines, I've thrown a leg over a fair number of bikes, and while these days I occasionally have a hard time remembering where I left my car keys, I can remember at least one day on every one of those bikes.

The last issue of *Retro* I saw had an article about the Yamaha RD-350. I have a lot of history with Yamaha twins, starting with an R5, and including an RD350 and several 250cc roadracers, all of which I rode in either AFM or AMA races, or both.

Just seeing the pictures in the article brought good memories flooding back. But I'm pretty sure that to ride any of those bikes now would only disappoint me. And since I still don't have room for a museum in my house, I'll just stick with the one in my mind.

Rookie Fever

(2001)

They say you can't go home again. I say you can, but sometimes you need a guide.

Let's say you're trying to recapture the magic of the time when you started riding, the feeling of wonder that accompanied even the smallest discoveries, like the first time you leaned way over into a corner and didn't die, or the day your instincts overcame your fear and you grabbed the front brake *hard* and came to a stop so quickly you almost couldn't get your feet down fast enough. You *can* get that sense of wonder back again. All you have to do is ride with a rookie.

A buddy of mine from a long way back recently got in touch with me. The last time I'd seen him he was riding a Yamaha XS1 in bell-bottoms, a fringed leather jacket, and a Captain America helmet, all the height of style at the time. In the 25 years since then, he'd sold the Yamaha, gotten married, had a family, and moved three or four times. He had an office job with a big company in a big city, and a lot more gray hair than anyone his age should have had, and now he was as happy as a kid who'd just gotten his first kiss. He was getting another motorcycle.

The next day he flew to Los Angeles and met a mutual friend of ours. Together they went to see a bike the friend had found. My buddy liked it, bought it, and rode it home—about 1200 miles in two days. He was in a near panic most of the way, desperately searching for long-unused reflexes, and by the time he got home he was pretty well used up. The next morning, though, he was up at the crack of dawn, cautiously exploring the backroads near his house and grinning like a fool under his brand new full-coverage helmet, Captain America having long since been tossed out along with the bell-bottoms and the fringed jacket.

He called me again a few nights later to tell me about the ride he'd just come back from, in the eastern part of the state. "I didn't see a car for a hundred miles," he said. "Once I was on a road that went through miles and miles of wheatfields, just rolling off to the horizon. I stopped, took off my helmet, and just sat there, listening to the wind. It was *great!*" When he called, I was sitting in my home office, staring at a computer screen filled with a story I had no enthusiasm for writing. Suddenly I was out there beside that wheatfield with him, listening to the breeze ruffle the grass and feeling like I was the only person left on earth.

It occurred to me that I hadn't felt that way myself for longer than I could remember. The whole time he'd been away from bikes, I had barely stopped riding for more than a month or so at a time. It took his bubbling enthusiasm to remind me why I'd started riding in the first place. Things like rolling wheatfields, and solitude, and the sheer edgy joy of riding through the middle of nowhere with nothing between you and a long walk home but an improbably crude machine that didn't even have enough wheels to stand up all by itself without help.

A few weeks later we met for lunch at a place roughly equidistant from our home towns. I figured the distance, and time it should take, and pulled out of the driveway and into the restaurant parking lot within a couple of minutes of my schedule. My buddy was late, but he had a good excuse. He had rolled out of bed that morning before the sun came up and put about 200 miles behind him first. I got another version of the wheatfield story, but with mountains and snaky two-laners winding along the coast, delivered in the same breathless and awestruck style.

Practically speaking, he wasn't telling me anything I didn't already know. On a deeper level, though, he was reawakening me to the joy of riding, a feeling my veteran, been-there-done-that riding buddies and I don't talk about much, for fear it'll make us sound like rookies. It was then I realized what I'd lost, and what I'd just found again, thanks to my friend.

After lunch, we shook hands and he took off for home. I stood by my bike, checking my watch and figuring I could make it back in time for dinner. Then I thought about those wheatfields. I took my watch off, put it in my pocket, and covered the 75 miles back to the house in a little under 200 miles.

You Should Write A Book

(TREAD LIFE, 2009)

It's a fact of the human condition that nobody is ever satisfied with what they are, what they have, or what they look like. This is why magazine writers often aspire to write books.

It can't be for the money.

Some years ago I was approached by a publisher in Minnesota to write a book about high-performance Harleys. The editor there had gotten my name from the editor of one of the Harley magazines I write for. The magazine editor, having himself been a freelancer for many years, guessed or knew I was hurting for money, and nominated me for the book job. (He was also too smart to take on the job himself.)

I hadn't written a book of this type before. My two mystery novels were fiction, and fiction is marketed thus: First you write the book, then you see if anyone wants to publish it. The proposed Harley book was non-fiction, which is typically sold first, usually on the basis of an out-line, or assigned to someone who will produce a book to the publisher's specifications, then written.

The publisher that approached me specialized in car books—high-performance modifications, racing, history, how-to, that sort of thing. Someone there had decided to dip a toe into the Harley market, which at the time was robust and growing. None of the authors in their stable had any bike experience, so they went looking for someone who did, and found me.

After some back and forth about the style and the focus and the content, I signed a contract. I had six months to deliver a finished product, and was given an advance against royalties. That's a sum of money that's meant to tide an author over during the process of writing the book. When the book comes out, and royalties from sales start adding up, that money has to be "earned back" before the author gets any more. In other words, if the advance is $5000, the first $5000 in royalties the book earns go toward paying off the advance. After that, royalties come to the author in the form of actual money.

I started in on the book with the intention of doing my usual freelance work at the same time. That turned out to be harder than I thought. The book sucked up more and more of my time and, more important, my energy. Soon it began to suck up my bank account, too, as the advance ran out and no money came into replace it.

Along the way I grew frustrated with the Harley aftermarket. I'd have thought that calling up some company that makes wheels or engines or some other high-dollar part for Harleys and saying I'd like to put pictures of their products in my book would have elicited gratitude if not outright joy, and the prompt delivery of said pictures. Wrong.

You simply have no idea how hard it was to give away what amounted to free advertising. Some companies said they'd send art, then didn't. Others were suspicious. *What'll it cost us?* Nothing. *Really?* Really. *Well, I don't know...* One company rep got angry when I asked him to mail me slides of his product. He was upset about having to pay the postage. (Guess who didn't make it into the book.)

The book dragged on into its fifth, then its sixth month. The deadline passed. My editor gave me more time. He did it so casually I got the impression none of his authors ever met their deadlines. If they'd all had to go through what I was going through, it's a good bet they didn't.

I turned in the book two months late. By then I was more than willing to return to what I had previously thought of as the drudgery of my freelance magazine work. Several more months went by. Page proofs—photocopies of the book in its pre-press form—arrived. I read them, repaired the errors the in-house copyeditor had inserted, and sent them back.

About a year after I submitted the book, an advance copy appeared on my doorstep. It looked good. It could have been better—show me a writer who's written anything he thinks can't be improved, and I'll show you someone who's not really a writer—but it would do.

Prior to signing the contract to write the book, I had talked to my editor at length about projected sales, distribution, and a lot of other things that were relevant to how much money the book would earn me over the following years. I don't write for fun—not often, anyway—and if the project wasn't going to make a profit, I wasn't interested. I received a number of assurances that, in my innocence, I believed.

As it turned out, the book was a flop. It came out in October, right before the holiday season, a big time for booksellers. Except one of the big chain book stores went through a change of personnel at about the same time, and the new hire either forgot to order any copies of my book, or decided not to. At least that's the story I got from my editor.

Well, okay, I thought, we'll wait until next year. But by then, my book had been "mid-listed," bumped from the so-called front list of new books—despite no one having heard of it yet—and soon after it was effectively consigned to obscurity, otherwise known as the back list, which is one step above the table at the rear of the store marked "Any Book $2".

Eventually I learned that the company that published my book didn't much believe in advertising. They had a printed catalog, and a website, and after sending out a single round of press releases to enthusiast magazines, they figured their job was done. If they ever placed a paid ad for the book anywhere, I never heard about it.

A year of my life, and about $8000 of my own money, went into a book that is now genuinely rare. That's because last year I got a letter from the publisher saying my book was going out of print. No further copies would be printed—this was a given, since they still had thousands of copies left over from the original print run—and the ones on hand would be recycled. I could buy up the remainders at a reduced price and sell them myself, the letter went on, or they'd be happy to ship me two cases of books free of charge.

I asked for, and received, two cases of *Harley-Davidson Bolt-On Performance*, which sit in my garage unopened. Every time I go out to work on the V-Strom or go for a ride, I have to walk right past them. I could move them so I don't suffer that pang of regret the sight of them invariably triggers, but some publisher might call me someday and ask me to write a book, and I might say yes.

But believe me, that chapter of my life is over.

Remembrance Of Things Fast

(TREAD LIFE 2008)

I don't remember the first flattrack race I went to, but it was in the early 1970s. It was what they called Sportsman scrambles back then. The tracks had a hard-packed dirt surface, and were laid out in a rough oval, with at least one right-hander and a jump.

Scrambles were a staple of the Sportsman class, which had three levels, Novice, Junior, and Expert, with separate displacement categories within each. Sportsmen were amateurs who raced for tin—cheesy trophies with winged naked ladies on top, or engraved wooden plaques—mostly on converted enduros and the odd stripped-down street bike in the Novice ranks, and on serious track-only equipment in the Expert classes.

After you clawed your way to the top of the Sportsman ranks, you could get a Class C license and race in Nationals for money at big tracks like San Jose, the legendary mile oval next to the Santa Clara County Fairgrounds. But in Class C you went up against hard, hungry, card-carrying professionals instead of the dog walkers, paper boys, and other weekend racers you'd been playing around with until then.

In Hayward, California, there was a small, beat-up, roach motel of a scrambles track I grew to love like my own home. It had a long back straight with a jump in the middle of it that funneled into a decreasing-radius left-hander bordered by a chain-link fence, which was all that kept the racers and the spectators apart. Then the right-hander, a short straight, a shallow right followed by a 180-degree left, and onto the straight again.

The fence along the back straight was made of plywood, and was painted with ads for local bike shops, burger joints, and gas stations. The chain-link fence outside the left-hander bulged toward the stands like a catcher's mitt, deformed by the repeated impact of riders who misjudged their entry speed, or got high-sided into it by someone passing on the inside.

The track was lined with yellow sodium lights that made it look like a Safeway parking lot at night, which was when most of the races were held. The pits were as dark as the inside of a cow.

The 250 Novice class was more competitive, and a whole lot more fun to watch, than the name would suggest. The 250s and the 650s— mostly big, bucking, thundering BSAs and Triumphs—were what the fast guys rode, both in Sportsman and later in the pros.

The races to watch on any given night were 250 Novice and Expert, and 650 Novice and Expert. The 250 Novice races were like little league baseball, where gaping holes in experience were plastered over with enthusiasm. The 650 Novices were just more of the same, except the bikes were faster, noisier, and a lot harder to control. The Expert races in either category were simply wonderful, cut-throat duels between masters of the craft.

But it was San Jose that turned my infatuation with flattrack into hopeless adoration. They called it The Mile. When you said it, everyone knew which mile you were talking about. Nothing I had ever seen prepared me for the first time I stood on the outside of turn one, my fingers laced in the chain-link fence, as a pack of riders appeared first as tiny dots in the shimmering heat coming up off faraway turn four.

They came barreling down the front straight, chins on the tanks and left hands gripping the fork tubes, the roar of voices in the grandstands marking their progress, the confused knot of bikes and riders dissolving into discrete shapes, jockeying for position, darting this way and that, testing, probing, drafting.

As they separated into Brelsford and Scott and Rayborn and Mann, the frantic thunder of the unmuffled engines rose to a shattering roar. Then one by one the riders snapped the throttles shut, dropped steel-shod boots off stubby pegs onto the track, slick and black with rubber, the famed "blue groove," began feeding in the throttle again, balancing the rear tire on the knife edge separating traction and disaster, blowing by one after the other with a concussive *wham wham wham* like the shock wave of jets flying right on the deck, the sound rocking me back, then fading, fading, until they disappeared down the back straight, leaving me standing on wobbly knees, as dazed and euphoric as a teenager after his first kiss.

I never forgot that feeling, and I hope I never do. The Mile is gone now. So is Hayward, and Fremont, Hall's Ranch, and Ascot, where I once saw Mert Lawwill lean his Harley over so far in turns one and two that when he picked it up again for the back straight there was dirt on his left number plate.

I went to the last Ascot half-mile, on September 29, 1990, and took along a wooden-handled garden trowel and an apothecary jar in a backpack. After the main event was over, and the riders were rolling their bikes back to the pits for the last time ever, I dug a big divot out of the fast line in turn one, took it home, and put it on the shelf next to another jar with a slice of The Mile's blue groove, in which the imprint of tire tread was still visible.

There aren't any flattrack races in the part of the country where I live now, and I haven't found the time to travel to any others, so I haven't been to one in years. But any time I want to remember what it was like, all I have to do is look at those jars of dirt. And even if I never see another flattrack race, well, I'll always remember San Jose.

Road Food

In 1952, when I was born, the second World War was still fresh in the American collective memory. It was so fresh, in fact, that while I lay diapered and talcumed in my crib, absorbed with the task of fitting my entire foot in my mouth (at which I wouldn't become truly proficient until years later, when I became a writer), there were men in my neighborhood afraid to go to sleep at night lest their dreams carry them back to bloody beaches on the Normandy coast, or shallow foxholes on some nameless Pacific island, or the cramped nose of a B-24 flying through thick bursts of flak.

When I was old enough to read, among the books I found in my house was one called *Up Front* by Bill Mauldin, who was a cartoonist during WWII for the Army newspaper *Stars & Stripes,* and a political cartoonist after that. The book was illustrated with cartoons of Mauldin's archetypal dogfaces, Joe and Willie, whose travails taught me many strange things I would have no context for until years later, such as the fact that the Russians—the hated and feared enemies of my Cold War childhood—had once been our allies. Another was the soldiers' distaste for the C-ration, a packaged combat meal containing technically food-like substances that could be eaten in the field without consequences more serious than, say, a flesh wound. Between the time Joe and Willie returned to civilian life and now, the C-ration morphed into the MRE, an acronym for "meal, ready to eat," a term which many of today's vets say is three lies in one.

The MRE and I met when I was getting ready for a long ride through some fairly desolate territory. My low-blood-sugar alarm goes off like an air-raid siren—one second I'm fine, and the next I'm starving—so instead of trusting I'll find a restaurant when I get hungry, I carry food with me. I had tried snack food, and granola bars, and found them wanting as complete meals. So I went to a sporting goods store to see what sort of things hunters took with them, and discovered the civilian version of the MRE. They were on sale for three dollars each, so I bought four, one each of several varieties. Later that day I ate one for lunch. It wasn't bad. It wasn't a nice sit-down meal in a roadside café, but it didn't take an hour, or cost 10 bucks, and the service was great.

I'm not prepared to say that a great dining experience awaits within the olive-drab-green plastic pouch. But having had some truly awful meals on the road, some of which continued to haunt me for days afterward, I'm reminded of what a buddy of mine who traveled the dirt-track circuit once said about McDonalds. "It's shitty food," he said, "but it's *consistently* shitty." This was a back-handed compliment to the homogeneity of the menu, which unlike that at a no-name greasy spoon is unlikely to make you sick. The same is true for MREs, which can withstand high storage temperatures, and have a shelf-life that's measured literally in years.

For a while I was embarrassed to admit I carried MREs with me.

Some of my riding buddies are into high-tech power bars and energy food sticks that have been field-tested on the slopes of the Himalayas, and they wash them down with special drinks containing rare minerals and electrolytes and the precious bodily fluids of giant deep-sea squid. On one ride, however, we pulled into a rest area on the interstate, and what began as a quick comfort stop turned into a lunch break.

My buddies broke out the astronaut food and began munching like goats eating old mattresses. Meanwhile I walked over to a picnic table, cut open an MRE, and laid out pasta and vegetables, applesauce, strawberry jam and crackers, a chocolate-covered cookie, powdered orange drink, and a bag with condiments, a plastic spoon, and a wet-nap for cleaning up. The munching sound ceased, and soon my buddies were gathered around the picnic table, drooling like starving dogs outside a butcher's shop. Suddenly I was back in the third grade, eating my lunch out of a paper bag, and being asked if I wanted to trade my Snickers for an orange.

Just as food eaten around a campfire tastes better than food eaten in a kitchen, an MRE's appeal is location-dependent. On my most recent long ride, from Boise, Idaho, back to the Oregon coast, I suddenly hit the hunger wall on a two-laner between I-5 and the coast, miles from anywhere. The weather was threatening rain, and I needed calories to face the cold and finish the ride.

I pulled into a rest stop and laid out an MRE on top of the trunk lid. It wasn't the surf 'n' turf platter, but nothing I had ever found at the bottom of a saddlebag tasted as good on that rainy afternoon in the middle of nowhere.

And I didn't even have to get shot at.

The Hole Truth

(AMERICAN RIDER)

I took a ride from Coos Bay to Seattle last year. It was a trip I won't soon forget, but only partially because of the fun I had once I got there. It was the getting there and back that'll be hard to forget.

I made it a two-day ride on the way there, and on the first night, just before I turned it, I checked the bike over and found a large nail in the rear tire, along with barely enough air to keep the rim off the pavement. I had a flat-repair kit with me, and a small 12-volt air compressor, and fixed the tire in about 10 minutes.

The next morning I checked it again before setting out, and it was holding air. Still, I stopped twice along the way, and added air once. About an hour from that night's stop it began to rain so hard that at first I couldn't see the car in front of me, then I couldn't see my own speedometer. There was so much water on the road I could have had two flat tires and I wouldn't have known it.

About 10 miles from the motel the rear end suddenly lurched to

one side, so I pulled over onto the shoulder. The deluge notwithstand-
ing, traffic whizzed by inches from my left foot. I scrambled off the right
side of the bike, kicked the rear tire a couple of times—not so much out
of frustration as to see if it felt flat or not—decided it wasn't flat—yet—
and rode to the next exit where I got soaked to the skin examining the
tread surface. Just as I got ready to go I thought to check the front, and
found the broken end of a box-knife blade embedded deep in the center
of the tread. Holding my breath I pulled it out. No leak, so I scooted for
the motel.

A friend met me there in his car and we proceeded to one of the
events that had brought me to Seattle. When he dropped me off later,
the rear tire was as flat as a Big Twin torque curve. I had picked up a
second nail in the 10 miles since I last checked it. I plugged the hole,
aired it up, and went to sleep that night wondering just what the hell else
I'd find in the morning.

Now, for various reasons I don't need to go into, this adventure
happened not on the Heritage Softail loaner I intend to tell Harley I've
misplaced when they ask for it back, but another bike, one with—and
here's the important part—tubeless tires. It's important because as swell
as the Softie is, it came with spoked wheels, and tubes in its tires.

As you know if it's ever happened to you, if you puncture a tube-
type tire, you are severely screwed. If you're lucky, that can of flat-fix
goo you've had in the saddlebag since you bought the bike hasn't hard-
ened into a material resembling the stuff they make billiard balls out of.
If you're not lucky, you're going to have to remove the tube and patch
it, and to do that you're going to have to take the wheel off the bike. If
you had a quarter for every tool the average Harley rider carries, you
wouldn't be able to afford to call a tow truck, which is what you'd have
to do unless you were pulling a trailer with a lift and an air compressor.

Of course if you're very, very unlucky, you crashed when the tube deflated like a toy balloon, and you'll be too busy wondering if your Blue Cross is paid up to think much about how you're going to fix the flat.

I've traveled a fair bit on the Heritage, and I've managed to put the possibility of getting a flat while I'm on the road in a small, dark place, way in the back of my mind. I tell myself I have a cell phone, and a Motorcycle Towing Service membership, but lately I've gotten into the habit of turning on the cell at rest stops, and frankly I'm more than a little bit worried at all the places where its little red "no service" icon blinks at me.

As much as I'll miss the Heritage when the factory demands its return—or after my arrest for refusing to give it back, one or the other— I won't miss the spoked wheels. I've already asked for an Electra Glide or—cross your fingers for me—a Road King to replace it, but on one condition, that it has cast wheels and tubeless tires. Because as nice as the Softail's chromed spokers look, they'd look really ugly with flat tires on them.

Why Nothing Beats The Bike

(JALOPNIK, 2015)

"You race motorcycles?" the guy in the Mopar shirt said, moving away from me as if I were a bearded fanatic in a robe holding a sign predicting the imminent end of the world. "On pavement? You guys are fucking crazy!"

It wasn't the first time I'd heard that from a car guy, nor would it be the last. But what stuck with me was the person who said it drove Funny Cars.

Back then—around 1972 or so—Funny Cars were still morphing into what they are today. They were skittish, temperamental, nitrofueled, hold-my-beer-and-watch-this rocket sleds known for instantly and, without warning, disassembling themselves in a mushroom cloud of flame and smoking debris like one of those crackpot Acme devices that always failed spectacularly and left Wile E. Coyote wreathed in smoke and covered with charred fur.

This guy strapped himself into one of these things every Sunday afternoon and prayed he'd live to see Monday morning. But *I* was the crazy one.

The divide between car guys and bike guys was then, as it is now, as wide as the one separating dog owners and cat lovers, or football and baseball fans, and there was a time when I'd have agreed with the Mopar man. I was a car nut long before I ever rode a motorcycle. When I was a kid, the walls of my bedroom were plastered with photos of Jim Clark, Graham Hill, Bruce McLaren, and other Formula 1 greats of the 1950s and '60s. Under the bed where most kids hid their *Playboy*s I had copies of *Road & Track* with Rob Walker's F1 race reports. (The *Playboy*s were in the closet.) I had no idea who Mike Hailwood was, or Phil Read, or Giacomo Agostini. All I knew about motorcycles was traffic cops and hoods rode them.

Like many adolescent males entering their senior year of high school, I had a fully inflamed risk-taking gland and no way to reduce the swelling. Cars were beyond my financial reach, even the kind high-school kids drove in 1968. Then I thought, what about bikes? Around that time a friend offered to teach me how to ride on his three-speed Suzuki 120 in a parking lot. An hour later I was wobbling down the street missing shifts, stalling the engine at every light, and having the time of my short—and threatening to get shorter every minute—life.

Although motorcycles took center stage after that, I never fully got over cars. During the time I rode and raced bikes I autocrossed a couple of Capris, drove a few time-distance rallies using a Mickey Mouse watch and gas-station maps for navigation, and had a Sunbeam Tiger as a daily driver. But for the next three decades or so my adrenaline rush of choice came with two wheels, not four, and eventually motorcycles became not just my hobby but also my career.

These last few years, though, have seen old injuries get uppity and take a big chunk out of my former enjoyment of riding. Remembering the good times in the Tiger—like crossing the Golden Gate on a sunny day with the top down and a lovely lady friend in the other seat, and hitting 100 mph on the Richmond Bridge every morning on the way to work in Berkeley—I got a '99 Miata for those days when my back flared up at just the thought of slipping on my Roadcrafter, never mind actually riding a bike.

Over on Jalopnik.com you'll often hear "The answer is always Miata." If the question is "What's a cheap, fun substitute for a motorcycle?" then I'm inclined to agree. I don't have to wear a helmet or hi-viz armored clothes to drive it. If it's nice out I put the top down. If it's too hot or too cold I put it up and hit the a/c or the heater. It has a locking trunk, a spare tire, and a range of almost 300 miles. Maybe most important given the sorry state of my knees, it doesn't fall over at a stoplight if there's oil or gravel on the road.

It's no adventure bike—I've never taken it off pavement and never will, at least not on purpose—but driving it is an adventure. It's noisy and cramped, small and light. It can be steered almost by thought alone, and corners like a rat in a sewer pipe. A new set of sticky BF Goodrich tires ran me about what I used to pay for tires and installation for my GL1800, and will last a lot longer. My Miata has almost the same power-to-weight ratio as my old Tiger, which had a cast-iron 260-cubic-inch Ford V8 stuffed under the hood.

The safety advantage of cars hardly needs elaborating beyond noting that in 2006 I was in a 45-mph head-on collision with a pickup truck on a dark rural highway. If I'd been riding a bike instead of driving my airbag- and seatbelt-equipped Honda Civic, you probably wouldn't be reading this, and they'd still occasionally be finding pieces of me scattered along the shoulder of Libby-McClain Road.

Still, motorcycles are more compelling than cars for reasons having nothing to do with practicality or safety or economy. Anybody can drive a car. For cryin' out loud, my *mother* could drive a car. Most cars today can be driven—and often are—with half of the driver's brain cells idling in neutral. The consequences of screwing up are less than they've ever been, with seatbelts and airbags and crumple zones. In a few years you won't even have to drive the car; it'll do that for you. (Which, holy shit, if you want to get around in a vehicle you don't have to drive yourself, take the goddam bus.)

But riding a motorcycle requires your full and undivided attention because there's so much more at stake. The difference between an accident in a car and one on a bike can be the difference between a trip to the body shop and a ride in a body bag.

Riding takes a special set of skills, the chutzpah to give the Fates a stiff middle finger every time you hit the starter, and the nerve to put yourself in the line of fire, to suit up and go forth to ride the gauntlet of texting teens, sleepy soccer moms, weaving drunks, homicidal forest rats, bad roads, bad timing, bad judgment, and bad luck.

Despite starting out as a car guy, and driving one every day for mostly mundane reasons, I almost never dream about driving cars. I often dream about riding motorcycles. I'm at my best on a bike, balanced on the razor-thin line between a good day and a very, very bad one on two improbably small patches of rubber, with my senses and reflexes fully engaged. In those rare and transcendent moments when the bike and I are defying physics together like a single entity, I'm not thinking about work, or money, or what to have for lunch—I'm totally in the now, timeless and immortal.

It makes no sense, preferring the difficult and dangerous over the safe and convenient, but dammit, who says it has to? The hassle, the hazards, the unavoidable crap-your-pants moment—they're just part of the fun.

Hell, maybe they *are* the fun, which means that Funny Car guy was right, and I *am* fucking crazy. But if I am, here's why: Both cars and motorcycles get me where I'm going. But only motorcycles make me feel alive on the way.

The Best Job I Ever Had

(I wrote this in 2017 for a motorcycle website whose editor declined to publish it because he thought it was too critical of motorcycle websites. He was probably right.)

Thirty years ago I lost the best job I ever had, before or since. On June 12, 1987, *Cycle Guide* magazine closed its doors for good. That morning I rode to the seedy industrial park on Higgins Court in Torrance, parked my last-ever test bike in the garage, and took one last lap of the office. I paused at my cubicle, now empty of the helmets, jackets, press kits, and assorted debris that had washed up there in the last two-and-a-half years, and sat one last time in the chair in which I had often stared a hole in the wall willing an idea to come to me.

The guys who worked on the bicycle magazine in the other half of the building were as quiet as mourners at a funeral, knowing they'd still have jobs tomorrow while those of us on the motorcycle side wouldn't. Later that day the *Cycle Guide* staff gathered at a restaurant in Long Beach where stories were told, grievances aired, future plans laid out, and an immoderate amount of alcohol was consumed for that early in the afternoon.

I got my first full-time professional writing gig in 1984, with *Rider*. I managed to get fired from that job seven months later (on my birthday, too) and landed shortly thereafter at *Cycle Guide*, where I worked under people with degrees in journalism and English. They told me on my first day that if I worked my ass off and mastered what they taught me, when I left *CG* I'd take with me the necessary skills to make a living writing for anybody about anything. They were right, too.

I could use up half of the available space on the internet telling stories about how great it was to work at *CG* during the heyday of the print era—the new bikes I got paid to ride, my trip to France to try out the new Yamahas on Circuit Paul Ricard, interviewing Kenny Roberts on the dusty floor of the timing tower at Willow Springs and later that day riding a TZ750 around the track, and just generally—in the words of the late Charlie Everitt, who hired me for the job— "being treated as if I were a better person than I actually am."

All of that was great, but if I live to be a hundred I'll never forget the high of working with a staff of dedicated, quirky, funny, and freakishly talented enthusiasts to put out the best magazine we knew how. I've never had a job before or since where I worked as hard or laughed as much. Every month, when the new issue hit the stands, I felt like the proud parent of a precocious baby.

I was on vacation in Oregon, where I eventually moved, when I got word *CG* was closing down. I rushed back to the office in SoCal and faced the depressing task of putting out what we all knew was our last issue. We knew it, but for some reason we weren't allowed to say it in the magazine. Which really sucked, given what we'd all put into the title— I almost *died* for it, for fuck's sake. So we buried clues of our demise all through the issue because who cared if we got caught? What were they gonna do, *fire* us?

OK, Grandpa, we get it, you miss writing stories on a manual typewriter and mailing the magazine to readers via Pony Express. Everything was wonderful and magic in the past, and the present sucks. But it's actually better now, or haven't you heard of this new-fangled thing called the internet? Instead of four or five monthly magazines there are dozens of websites spewing out hundreds of stories a day. We get race results from the other side of the world before the checkered flag stops waving, and riding impressions of new models written and submitted so quickly that the bikes are still ticking as they cool down while we're reading about them.

What exactly was so great about dead-tree motojournalism—with content already three months out of date as soon as it arrived in the mailbox—that we should be sorry if it dies out?

Well, gather 'round, young 'uns, and I'll tell you a tale of a time when motojournos actually had time to think about what they were writing, to put it in some kind of big-picture context, fact check it, run it by the other staffers who'd point out errors and typos, and help polish a piece until it shined like the chrome on a new Harley, a process we called gang editing. A monthly magazine might not have flooded your brain with so much news your head swelled up like a balloon, but—with *CG* at least—what you got in return for less copy was better copy.

That's not always possible on the interwebs, where if your story pops up 10 minutes later than some other site's, you lose. It began with cable TV's 24-hour news cycle, where breathless, content-free **BREAKING NEWS** updates kept your eyeballs glued to the screen despite nothing newsworthy happening, which didn't matter as long as you hung in there for the commercials.

The internet is the small-screen version of that, and its insatiable appetite for content—any content, no matter how poorly written or irrelevant—increasingly sacrifices quality for quantity. When you're really hungry, you don't care too much how good the food is as long as it's filling. Chicken nuggets will do just as well as chicken cordon bleu.

Most of the motorcycle magazines that survive today are barely hanging on as readers—and more important, advertising dollars—migrate in droves to the web. Some have scaled back their page count, or their frequency, or changed up the content mix in an attempt to attract a new audience. I've worked for three titles that tried one or more of those things, and every one of them disappeared after a year or so. (As of this writing, a fourth is looking kind of shaky.)

All motorcycle magazines have websites that consume big chunks of staff time that would otherwise go into the print side, to the detriment of both. The two days you spend shooting a 10-minute video for the website are two days you can't spend polishing the magazine's feature road test, or editing a touring story, or riding a new bike. The internet is the biggest chick in the nest, working its parents to death fetching it more and more worms.

A former motojournalist who knows the downside of the digital revolution all too well told me that it's not just the website, but the entire digital footprint—web, social media, video—that makes it harder to put out a quality print product. Time spent on these projects forced him to "pre-write" some articles based on what was known prior to the event from marketing info or technical material, and then modify the article on the fly—or on the flight home—to suit what he learned later.

The need to make the print and online versions of the same story different meant twice as much work, he said, a situation made even worse by pressure to produce more and more click-baity content for the website without regard to its quality. His magazine underwent staff cuts and other money-saving measures ("Copyeditors? Proofreaders? Too expensive, cut 'em loose. *Fact checkers?* Ha!") while more and more energy was funneled to the website—which didn't, and probably still doesn't, turn a profit.

If you've ever bitched about motorcycle road tests reading like manufacturers' brochures, or all the magazines running essentially the same stories at the same time, with hardly any difference between the print and online versions, this is why. It's also why I'm still rambling on about the *CG* days 30 years later: I went freelance in 1988, when the World Wide Web was still just a twinkle in Tim Berners-Lee's eye, and never had to deal with this bullshit. And for that I'll always be grateful.

RIP *Cycle Guide*, 1967-1987. Here's looking at you, you magnificent paper-and-ink bastard. We'll always have Torrance.

About the Author

Jerry Smith has been a professional freelance writer for 30 years. You'd think he'd have found a real job in that much time, but no. Instead, he's written primarily for motorcycle magazines and websites, and for his own amusement, about motorcycles, riding motorcycles, writing about motorcycles, and sometimes about travel, dogs, and the highs and lows of writing for a living. He lives in Oregon with his editorial assistant and morale officer, a Golden Retriever named Dickens.

He has, despite his love of words on paper, been dragged into the 21st century and can be found on the web. To keep up with his writing and to purchase his other books, visit www.JerrySmithAuthor.com.

Made in the USA
Coppell, TX
28 February 2023

13521492R00115